Testim

In July of 2015, I was at my heaviest, 195 lbs… and I was engaged! I knew I needed a change—and fast. But, I am a police officer and I work long, exhausting, stressful nights. I didn't know if change was possible. Stacy Moutafis taught me how to create balance in my life. I learned to eat healthy with Stacy's meal prep techniques, and I trained with Stacy's vigorous Bridal Body workouts. With Stacy's coaching, I even learned to love the gym again! Today I stand fit and strong after losing a total of 37 lbs. and counting.

Erin Corcoran

I have struggled my entire life with an eating disorder and have always had a negative view on my body, that is, until I met Stacy Moutafis. When I first met Stacy, I was 20 lbs. overweight, had an active 3-year-old son and I was planning my dream wedding. I knew I wanted to look my best, but I also knew that starving myself was not the answer. I trusted Stacy's knowledge and believed that her Bridal Body meal plans and workouts would put me on a better, healthier path. By my wedding day, I lost 20 lbs. and was in the best shape of my life. I saw muscles I never knew I had! Most importantly, I achieved my goals the healthy way. I continue to follow Stacy's plans post wedding, pre-baby, and now post baby! Stacy has forever changed my life.

Nikita Bonamo

The countdown was on. Four months until my wedding. It was time to hit the gym, and that's where I met Stacy Moutafis (go figure!). I immediately inquired about her personal training sessions. Before I knew it, I was dedicated to her Bridal Body plan. She transformed my body and by my big day I was down 33 lbs.! Over the last ten years, Stacy has continued to work with me through many different life changes. She continues to motivate and inspire me.

Jennifer Gray

THE
BRIDAL BODY
BOOK

YOUR WORKOUT WORKBOOK
AND RECIPES FOR SUCCESS

By Stacy Moutafis

with Elisa DiStefano

MOtivational PRESS®
LEADERS IN GLOBAL PUBLISHING

Published by Motivational Press, Inc.
1777 Aurora Road
Melbourne, Florida, 32935

www.MotivationalPress.com

Manufactured in the United States of America.

ISBN: 978-1-62865-284-0

Contents

TESTIMONIALS 1

INTRODUCTION 9

STACY'S STORY 12

ELISA'S STORY 17

ELISA'S BRIDAL BODY JOURNAL 20

PART ONE 24

DIET DOS & DON'TS 31

PART TWO 40

SHOP WITH STACY 46

ELISA'S SURVIVAL TIPS 55

STACY'S WEEKLY PLAN PREP 57

TRAVEL TIPS 59

PART THREE 61

PART FOUR 72

FINAL COUNTDOWN 98

RECIPES 122

ACKNOWLEDGEMENTS 133

Because physical exercise can be strenuous and subject to risk of serious injury, Bridal Body LLC urges you to obtain a physical examination from a doctor before beginning any exercise or training program. You agree that by participating in these physical exercise sessions or personal training activities, you do so entirely at your own risk. This includes, without limitation, (a) your use of all amenities and equipment in the facility and any offsite location and your participation in any activity, class, program, personal training or instruction, (b) the sudden and unforeseen malfunctioning of any equipment (c) our instruction, training, supervision, or dietary recommendations. You agree that you are voluntarily participating in these activities and use of these facilities and premises and assume all risks of injury.

You expressly agree to release and discharge your personal trainer or instructor from any and all claims or causes of action. This waiver and release of liability includes, without limitation, all injuries to you which may occur, regardless of negligence.

If any portion of this release from liability shall be deemed by a Court of competent jurisdiction to be invalid, then the remainder of this release from liability shall remain in full force and effect and the offending provision or provisions severed here from.

You acknowledge that you have carefully read this waiver and release and fully understand that it is a release of liability. You agree to voluntarily give up any right that you may otherwise have to bring a legal action against the personal trainer or instructor for negligence, or any other personal injury or property damage or loss action.

___

To my beautiful, intelligent daughters, I dedicate this book to you. May your future be filled with love, prosperity, joy and may your wildest dreams come true. You inspire me every day to be the best I can be for you and for myself. Each of you own half of my heart. Love Mom

~ Stacy Moutafis

To my husband, the love of my life, who supported me every step of the way on my Bridal Body journey and continues to inspire me to be my best self, dream big and never be ordinary.

~ Elisa

To every bride, let this book be your guide to looking and feeling your bridal best, and may it be the first step on your path to a fit, healthy, and happily ever after.

~ Stacy & Elisa

Please find more fitness and nutrition tips, videos, recipes and Bridal Body products on our website BridalBodyBook.com.

Join in the conversation and share your #BridalBody journey on:

f **/BridalBodyBook**

○ **@BridalBodyBook**

🐦 **@BridalBodyBook**

𝓟 **/BridalBodyBook**

Introduction

I met Elisa DiStefano when she was working on a story about Miss Long Island (NY) Michelle Medoff. As Michelle's personal trainer and nutritionist, I prepare her for every pageant in which she competes. Elisa, who is a journalist and morning news personality, was filming and interviewing Michelle and me that day and was intrigued by Michelle's meal prep and the advice I had to offer regarding getting her in shape for her competitions.

We never know how meeting new people will change our lives, but I soon discovered that Elisa was discouraged by weight gain. She had tried a few diets and training protocols that simply didn't work. What was even more frustrating for Elisa was that she would soon be getting married and didn't feel she was in the best shape that she could be. After seeing what I could do for a competitor on the national stage, she wanted the same results. So, then and there, Elisa and I became partners on her journey to the best Bridal Body.

Chances are that if you picked up this book, you, too, have an upcoming wedding and want to look fit in your dress, as well as on your honeymoon. This book will do for you what I did for Elisa. I created a customized meal plan that was devised with her schedule, lifestyle, and goals in mind. From there, we met week to week (I have other clients who work with me via video chat) and spoke often on the phone. I adjusted her meal plan once she started losing the weight. I stuck close to Elisa the whole time as she expressed her concerns, her needs, and, yes, her frustrations. As her wedding day drew closer, I spoke to her almost every day. Then, we moved on to the final week, and then the day of her big event: marrying the love of her life. Elisa had lost over twenty-five pounds, her body fat percentage went from a thirty-three to a seventeen, and her dress size from a six to a zero. She did it the natural way, the healthy way, without cutting out any food groups or starving herself. She was a glowing and confident bride!

Working with sweet-natured Elisa, who was determined to lose weight, was a match made in heaven. Yet I know that my approach can work for every bride who wants to walk down the aisle feeling good about herself, which is why we were asked to share our information in this workbook. Elisa will contribute her journey as "the bride" while I will provide not only tips but a schedule and proven recipes that make sense for anyone who wants to feel and look great! This workbook is something to be kept nearby, a place to write your own journey, something to reference over and over again. But, first, congratulations on your upcoming nuptials; second, let's get you in your best shape possible for that very special day! Let's get you *your* Bridal Body!

Stacy Moutafis

Elisa & Stacy after a long evening of celebrating!

Stacy's Story

STRENGTH DOESN'T COME FROM WHAT YOU CAN DO. IT COMES FROM OVERCOMING THE THINGS YOU ONCE THOUGHT YOU COULDN'T.

As we begin this journey together, I want you to have complete confidence in my personal training and coaching abilities. I also want you to get to know me and my story of passion and perseverance.

My work ethic stems from my hard-working immigrant family. My love of athletics comes from my father, a professional soccer player and coach. As a child growing up on the East End of Long Island, New York, I pretty much played every sport and was a competitive high school cheerleader. I enjoyed being an athlete, and fitness was always an interest of mine; so imagine how devastating it was when I was diagnosed with a giant cell tumor in my leg at just eighteen years old.

I had to give up the sports I loved to spend three years recovering from seven reconstructive knee surgeries. If it weren't for Dr. Samuel Kenan at the Hospital for Joint Diseases in Manhattan, I could have lost my leg. Dr. Kenan did a femur reconstruction. I was told that most of my range of motion and abilities would be forever limited, if not totally gone. Needless to say, I was depressed, hopeless, and of course in a lot of pain for three years. Rehabilitation was a major turning point in my life. I began to really understand just how important exercise and muscular development truly were. This realization inspired me to become a personal trainer and therapist, and motivated me to want to help others. Nothing gives me more fulfillment than watching my clients progress and feel better—especially those like me, who were told they couldn't achieve their goals.

As my body strengthened, I wanted to take my own personal fitness journey further. I began competing as a figure and fitness athlete, performing on a national stage. For someone considered "legally disabled" just a few years prior, it was to the amazement of many that I became a Top 5 National Level Competitor and competed in the industry for an unprecedented thirteen years.

After an expected win, Stacy earned a heartbreaking 4th place finish at the NPC Team Universe National Fitness Championships due to the technical difficulty of her music being disrupted. She still considers it to be the best show experience of her career.

Stacy performs what she considers the best routine of her competition career at the 2009 NPC Team Universe Fitness Championships

Some say it was my determination or competitive spirit; I say it was my love of fitness and my obligation to inspire every single person who felt like they were in some way impaired.

I am certified to work with both amateur and professional athletes of all ages. I've trained everyone from television and radio personalities to pageant contenders, police officers, the U.S. military, and, of course, brides-to-be.

As a mother of two young girls, my goal is to inspire all children to develop healthy habits from an early age. I am especially passionate about working with families, and I also specialize in prenatal fitness.

I've appeared in many magazines and on television and radio shows, sharing weight loss tips and healthy recipes.

Known nationally for my weight loss transformations, as well as strength and conditioning coaching, I have the following certifications:

- ISSA Personal Trainer
- ISSA Strength and Conditioning Coach
- ISSA Fitness Therapist
- ISSA Sports Nutrition Specialist
- YogaFit Instructor
- Licensed Food Manager

Elisa's Story

THE BODY ACHIEVES WHAT THE MIND BELIEVES...

It was January 2014, the beginning of my "wedding year". It was supposed to be the happiest time of my life, but I was depressed—distraught, really. I had put on twenty pounds to my 5'1" frame since my engagement six months prior—months of celebrating, dining out, oh, and all that champagne! Instead of hitting the gym, I was spending my little free time with my fiancé. We had wedding plans to make! I'll never forget the moment on New Year's Eve when I realized I barely recognized myself after all this making merry. I hated how I looked, and worse, how I felt. My weight became a major distraction. I wasted so much energy worrying about it, being upset about it. I even refused to try on wedding dresses. I needed more than a New Year's resolution. I needed help, and fast, with the wedding just months away.

That's when I feel the Universe brought me Stacy Moutafis. She changed my life! She taught me about nutrition, my own body, and even how to cook, which is perhaps my biggest accomplishment to date! We set goals. We worked hard. I was feeling good and could see the results. More importantly, on my wedding day, I was my best self. And even *more* importantly, Stacy has helped me sustain this healthy new lifestyle and keep the weight off. I am now inspired and committed to helping other brides-to-be.

The day we met, courtesy of Michelle Medoff!

Our wedding day at Oheka Castle, Long Island NY

Planning a wedding is stressful enough . Let us take this part (and wait until you see what else!) off your plate. The best tip that I can give you is that even if your wedding seems far away, start working on your Bridal Body NOW! I reached my goal the month before my wedding day, and thank goodness I did, because the wedding month is so busy that all bets are off. Wouldn't you want to know well in advance that the dress you spent a ton of money on will look beautiful on your fit Bridal Body? To keep me on track, Stacy had me keep a journal.

Elisa's Bridal Body Journal

WEDDING DATE: August 28, 2014

This gives me 7 (seven) months until I take those vows.

My starting weight: 142 pounds

New Year's Eve — the beginning of my wedding year 2014, when I realized a change had to be made

FITNESS GOALS:

- Lose 20 (twenty) pounds
- Be stronger
- Shrink arms
- Flatten belly
- Say goodbye to fat
- Feel better
- And, oh yes, fit into my spring clothes (I'm on a wedding budget, after all!)

It certainly looks impressive on paper, right? But Stacy didn't sugarcoat anything and wanted me to consider what all my obstacles would be in reaching those goals. I had to be honest with Stacy and myself, and not make excuses—but make changes.

ELISA'S OBSTACLES:

- Time

I wake up at 2:30 a.m. every day for work and put in long hours. In addition, I am involved in many activities.

- Meal Prepping

I don't cook often and have no idea how to prepare the recipes I need to help get me in shape. I am unsure of how much to eat or even when I should be eating, since my schedule is not the same as the average nine-to-five person's schedule.

- Social Life

I have many networking lunches and social functions, and dine out often.

My list is here to show that everyone has obstacles—some may be the same for you, while others are unique to each bride-to-be.

I was motivated to work through these obstacles because my time was ticking, and I needed to get shopping for "the dress."

LET'S GET STARTED!

To Get Started You Will Need:

1. A food scale

2. Measuring cups and measuring spoons

3. Plenty of containers

4. Small cooler bag and ice packs

5. Water bottle

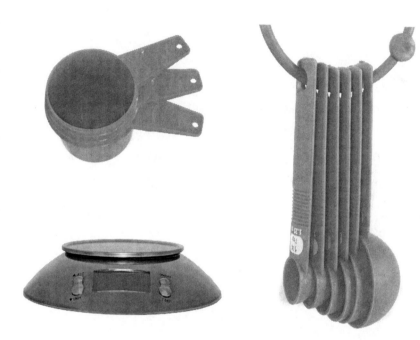

Part One

*F*irst things first. Let's talk about "the dress". The end goal for so many of you, in addition to living a new, healthy lifestyle, is to look your bridal best in your wedding dress.

If you follow The Bridal Body Book, you will have a Bridal Body transformation. But for now, let's work with what you've got, because unless you are buying off the rack, you have to order your dress months in advance.

So many brides choose the wrong dress for their body type. For many of you, this is the one dress you've been dreaming about your entire life. But here's the reality: That dream dress may not be the most flattering on you.

Let's look at your current body assets to choose the best dress for your body.

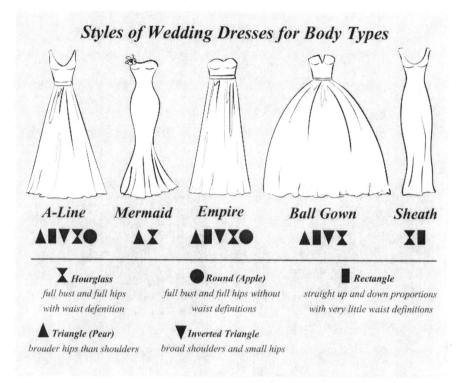

Styles of Wedding Dresses for Body Types

A-Line	Mermaid	Empire	Ball Gown	Sheath
▲▮▼✕●	▲✕	▲▮▼✕●	▲▮▼✕	✕▮

✕ **Hourglass**
full bust and full hips with waist defenition

● **Round (Apple)**
full bust and full hips without waist definitions

▮ **Rectangle**
straight up and down proportions with very little waist definitions

▲ **Triangle (Pear)**
broader hips than shoulders

▼ **Inverted Triangle**
broad shoulders and small hips

Once you've said yes to the dress, you have to look your best in it. There's no fairy godmother here. You have to work hard—and smart.

The Bridal Body workouts you'll find in this book will tone and transform your ENTIRE body.

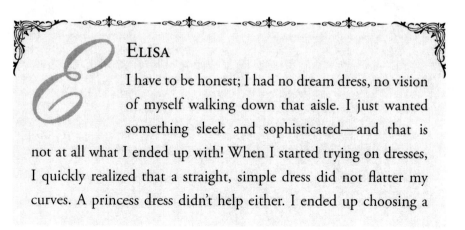

ELISA

I have to be honest; I had no dream dress, no vision of myself walking down that aisle. I just wanted something sleek and sophisticated—and that is not at all what I ended up with! When I started trying on dresses, I quickly realized that a straight, simple dress did not flatter my curves. A princess dress didn't help either. I ended up choosing a dress that was fitted on top and through the waist with volume on the bottom to balance my curves. Here's a tip—pick a dress you love at the weight you are at now. Trust me, you'll love it even more when you are looking and feeling your bridal best!

Elisa selecting the right dress for the big day!
The Wedding Salon of Manhasset, Long Island NY

Elisa said yes to this dress!

and then had her Bridal Body transformation.

Let's get to your Bridal Body goals, BRIDE-TO-BE!

BRIDE'S NAME:_____

WEDDING DATE: _____

LOCATION: _____

STARTING WEIGHT: _____

Insert your photo here in this blank space:

BODY TYPE:_____

DRESS STYLE RECOMMENDED:_____

DRESS STYLE SELECTED:_____

OBSTACLES:_____

Track your Bridal Body progress by beginning your Bridal Body worksheet on Page 121.

Diet Dos & Don'ts

You are what you eat, so don't be fast, cheap, easy or fake.

Dishing on Diets

Okay, so here it is, the real dish on dieting fads and these so-called weight loss solutions. I've been using a standard protocol for so many years successfully, and I believe it works best because it is balanced, with no real restrictions, and is just a healthy way to live. I always say that you cannot out-exercise bad nutrition, so let's get it straight.

No Carb—No Way!

Poor carbohydrates; they are the most misunderstood macronutrient. Over the years, carbs have been identified as the reason for weight gain, causing the carb-free craze. But carbohydrates are your number one energy source providing fuel to your body. Here's what you need to understand about carbs:

Starch carbs, also known as complex carbohydrates, are the carbs that are digestible. They produce four calories per gram eaten. They are your main source of energy every day. The GOOD carbohydrates are in natural forms and do not overload your blood sugar with glucose. They are typically low-glycemic and non-processed. Excess glucose or glycogen, when unused, turns to fat. The correct amount of carbohydrate intake is vital to your health, weight loss, and athletic performance.

Simple sugars, or simple carbohydrates, come in the forms of fructose and glucose. These are usually found in sweets, processed convenience foods, sports drinks, and many other processed foods. These are usually high-glycemic and can be blamed for that "daily crash" or sugar craving that most of us get midday. This is normally caused by a rush of sugar into the blood stream that does not last, causing a spike in insulin levels.

Veggies are also forms of carbohydrates. They are fibrous in nature and hold only one to two calories per gram. They are less digestible than starch carbs and do not affect blood sugar levels the same way as starch carbs do, as long as they are in their natural forms.

Fruits are also carbohydrates, in that they provide energy to the body. They are also vitamin-packed and provide a great source of antioxidants. However, be careful with fruits—they also provide a high number of calories and sugar grams per ounce.

What Is the Glycemic Index?

The glycemic index is an index used worldwide that is based upon how quickly sugar (glycogen) enters the blood after certain foods are eaten.

All forms of carbohydrates fall somewhere on the glycemic index. Your meal plan will have a specific carbohydrate-gram goal per meal and per day to ensure the proper intake to reach your goals.

Warning: If you restrict your carbohydrate intake, your body will rely on proteins and fats for fuel. This can lead to a loss of lean body mass, irritability (not good for a happy bride-to-be), and other problematic issues.

BUT the scale says...

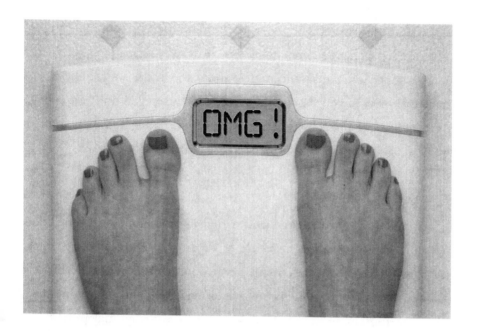

Here's where it gets tricky—carbs carry about three molecules of water for every gram ingested, so when you stop the carbs, your scale says you lost weight. But guess what? You have not lost FAT, you have lost WATER. The correct process of losing weight is ingesting the right amount of each macronutrient for your individual needs.

Pass the Protein!

I could go on and on about the *power of protein*, which has so many benefits, but I will try to keep this short! This powerhouse macronutrient helps burn calories while you digest it! Enough said. Not really, here's more: It also repairs muscle tissue, creates hormones, aids in blood production, and is what we need to sustain our current lean body mass. PLUS protein, unlike carbohydrates, does not affect blood sugar levels. When eaten with carbs, it actually neutralizes that glycemic effect, thereby slowing down your glucose response so that you stay nutritionally satisfied and are less likely to crave simple sugars.

So, is there such thing as too much protein? There is. But there are also adverse effects when not enough has been eaten. Because protein's function is to build, repair, and sustain muscle and tissue in the body, these crucial structural parts of your body can be sacrificed when you don't eat enough protein. Exercise and activity level play a role in deciding how much protein we need, as well as an estimation of your existing lean body mass.

TYPES OF PROTEIN

Animal Protein (meat and poultry): This protein is highly metabolic, meaning it burns calories in order to digest it. Lean cuts of red meat (such as filet mignon and sirloin) are recommended. But chicken and turkey (without skin) are less fatty than red meats and offer you a lean complete protein source. I do recommend *organic* animal proteins to avoid pesticides, hormones, and antibiotics.

Fish: All fish, with the exception of salmon, mackerel, and blue fish (since their fat content is either equal to or greater than protein content) is considered protein. If you are not allergic to fish, please consume it! Most fish are low caloric and offer omega-3 fatty acids that have many benefits to your heart, cholesterol, and brain function. My advice is not to ingest farm-raised fish, since it grows in a controlled environment where man can make alterations to its quality.

Eggs and Egg Whites: Egg whites offer a natural source of protein and can be considered one of nature's best! Naturally having all essential amino acids and NO fat, egg whites are a great protein source. Full eggs with the yolk are good as well, but beware of those five to six grams of saturated fat that come with eating a full egg; those grams can add up. Organic eggs are highly recommended. Egg whites in cartons are usually preserved with chemicals and are not recommended.

Whey Protein: Whey is a derivative of dairy. It is fast-acting and, unless compromised by additives and preservatives, an excellent source of protein.

Soy Protein: Soy is a derivative of a soybean. It is the part of the bean that provides protein. Unlike animal-based proteins, it lacks essential amino acids; therefore it is not recommended as your main protein source. ** Vegetarian-based diets would include higher levels of soy protein than others.

Protein Imposters!

Protein bars: Believe it or not, these are highly processed and offer limited amounts of protein. They are usually highly caloric and full of sugar.

Deli Meat: Processed, preserved, and just not quality protein. Deli meats are also high in sodium and sugar. This includes culprits like turkey bacon and processed meats like sausage and pork products.

Your Daily Dairy

First, I'd like to point out the benefits of dairy. Dairy is rich in calcium and, if low-fat, contains the building blocks casein and whey, which are highly effective protein sources. Because dairy has a reputation of being filled with antibiotics, hormones, and pesticides, I am very careful when recommending it to clients. If choosing dairy, I strongly suggest consuming organic only.

*** Because dairy has been proven to aid in mucus production, those with allergies and chronic sinus conditions are not recommended to ingest dairy.

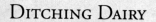

Ditching Dairy

I loved dairy! I'd start every day with (low-fat) creamer in my coffee and tons of milk with cereal. Yogurt or frozen yogurt was my favorite mid-day snack. And, I would often ask "pass the cheese, please!" and then add it (just a bit) to everything! For weight loss, and because I had a thyroid issue, the first major change I (with Stacy's suggestion) made was taking dairy out of my diet. I now only have almond or coconut milk. My big, bloated stomach deflated, and my stomach issues disappeared, as well! Here's the most amazing thing to me: After just one year of changing how and what I eat, my thyroid levels evened out and I am now off my thyroid medication.

FAT-FREE—NOT FOR ME!

Here's the skinny on FAT. Fat is a powerful macronutrient that everyone needs. You need fats to live, function… and lose weight. Fat burns fat. Yep, I said it. With nine calories per gram, fat causes your metabolism to work hard, in turn burning more calories. Fats fuel your body with Vitamins A, D, E, and K. Fats aid in brain function and cell development, and are your secondary energy source. When you run out of carbs, your body relies on fats ingested and stored to fuel daily activities. Twenty-five percent of your caloric intake should come from good, healthy fats.

THE GOOD, THE BAD, AND THE UGLY FATS

So what are the "good" fats? Good fats offer quality fats, such as omega-3 and omega-6 fatty acids. They are not saturated and are said to increase HDL, good cholesterol. Good fats come from natural sources such as nuts, olive oil, flax, hemp, avocado, fatty fish, and natural nut butters. For fat loss, a healthy diet should take at least twenty percent of its total calories from good, healthy fats.

The "bad" fats, saturated fats, are found in most fatty animal proteins and hydrogenated vegetable oils. They can also be found in most fatty processed foods. They cause an increase in bad cholesterol, LDL, and are said to be part of the cause of heart disease. They have little biological function and supply a high level of unwanted calories.

Because fats are so caloric, your metabolism has to work harder to process these macronutrients than any other. It will burn more calories in doing that, as well as have an effect on blood sugar levels. During the process of fat loss, I suggest NOT combining starch carbs with fats because of the affects on blood sugar levels.

For example, peanut butter on a slice of toast.

Bread - Starch carb

Peanut Butter - Fat

So, the combination is a double whammy on your body and a big no-no—adding jelly makes is a no-no-no! If you absolutely have to have it, add a protein, such as whey or egg white, and that will, in turn, slow down the effects on blood sugar levels. * Remember, protein is a neutralizer.

Here's what can happen if you restrict your healthy fat intake:

- **Poor Vitamin Absorption:** Vitamins A, D, E, and K will not be utilized properly since they are fat-soluble vitamins, which will lead to low bone density. It will affect your hair and skin.

- **Depression:** You will be emotional enough as you prepare for your wedding! A diet that is too low in fat will hurt your mental health. Omega-3s and omega-6s play a role in mood and behavior, since they are the precursor of many hormones and chemicals produced in the brain.

- **Increased Cancer Risk:** Breast and prostate cancer have both been linked to low-fat diets that lack essential fatty acid.

- **Increased Risk for Heart Attack:** Not eating enough good fatty acids will promote a low level of HDL, which is your hyper lipoprotein's good cholesterol that fights off heart disease.

- **Macronutrient Imbalance:** If you're not eating enough fat, you're bound to eat too many carbohydrates. This can lead to a blood sugar elevation and increased craving of sugar.

- **Overeating Bad Food:** If you opt for a low-fat label or fat-free propaganda, it usually means that more chemicals, preservatives, and sugar alcohols are hiding in those foods. These factors will eliminate the process of fat metabolism and weight loss.

CHEERS… TO NO ALCOHOL

You're the bride. I get it, you need a drink every once in a while. Keep in mind, we consume an average of 400 calories in alcohol at a party—that's 400 empty calories—calories that are just sitting around, ready to be stored as fat. Don't forget, alcohol is a depressant. Depressed is not what you want to feel when you are focused on your weight loss and wedding! And if you are still not convinced, alcohol is full of chemicals, nitrates, and preservatives, killing any nutritional value of, say, that recommended one glass of red wine a day. (Oh, and don't forget the staining of your pearly whites!) I call alcohol the biggest muscle killer around. Because of those chemicals and high levels of nitrates, anything that's fermented will destroy any lean body mass it comes in contact with. So, like I said, cheers to NO alcohol.

Just Add Water

And lots of it. Before we get into exercise, make sure you have a water bottle ready. Any exercise or sport activity lasting over an hour will generally increase your water need by fifty percent. Water replenishment should take place immediately before, as well as during and after exercise.

Part Two

IF IT DOESN'T CHALLENGE YOU, IT DOESN'T CHANGE YOU.

Stacy & I spent many hours in her office discussing my food plans- and we still do!

Getting Started

I found getting started to be the hardest part. For me this wasn't just a wedding diet, it was a huge change in lifestyle and a new way of life. I encourage you to embrace the change! As you make this investment in yourself, you must also invest in a few key items.

Items needed:

❀ A Food Scale

Weight matters. As you start your Bridal Body transformation, it's actually more important to weigh your food than it is to weigh yourself! I had no idea what three ounces of chicken was until I bought my food scale. It's not just about eating the right food; it's also about eating the right amount of those foods. Make sure you also have plenty of other measuring tools like cups and spoons!

TIP: Weigh your food once it is cooked—not raw or frozen!

❄ Containers

Too bad Tupperware parties aren't trendy these days, because I sure bought a lot of it! Invest in good food storage containers that seal shut and fit together to stack and store easily, because you are going to use it every day. While you are at it, get plenty of sandwich bags, ice packs, and a good cooler bag. You'll soon be taking it with you everywhere!

❄ Water bottle

You are going to be drinking a lot of water. Get a water bottle you like carrying around. Stacy gave me a water bottle that holds my daily gallon water requirement so that I could keep—and stay—on track!

❄ Blender

It's so much easier if you buy a blender that can make a single serving in a to-go cup (with a lid). It will help making your protein shakes a pleasure!

YOU CAN'T EXPECT TO LOOK LIKE A MILLION BUCKS
IF YOU EAT FROM THE DOLLAR MENU.

TIME TO CLEAN OUT YOUR CABINETS (but first, read this)

So here's the deal: You can't believe everything you read, especially on the front of food packages. Manufacturers can say anything they want on the front label, so to get the real story, you have to read the nutrition facts panel on the back.

Below are some terms to look for and know what they really mean.

Fortified, enriched, added, extra, and plus—Nutrients such as minerals and fiber have been removed, and vitamins have been added in processing.

Tip: Look for 100 percent whole-wheat bread and high-fiber, low-sugar cereals.

Fruit drink—There's probably little or (gasp!) no real fruit, but instead, lots of sugar.

Tip: Look for products that say "100% fruit juice".

Made with wheat, rye, or multigrain—These products may have very little whole grain.

Tip: Look for the word "whole" before the "grain" to ensure you're getting a 100 percent whole-grain product.

Natural—The manufacturer started with a natural source, but once it's processed, the food may not resemble anything natural.

Tip: Look for "100% All Natural" and "No Preservatives".

Organically grown—pesticide-free or no artificial ingredients

Tip: Only trust labels that say "Certified Organically Grown".

Sugar-free or fat-free—Do not assume this means that the product is low-calorie. The manufacturer may have compensated with unhealthy ingredients that don't taste very good and have NO FEWER CALORIES than the real thing.

Tip: Avoid sugar-free or fat-free labeling.

There are also some phrases on the nutrition facts panel that you should be aware of:

Serving Size—Portion control is important for weight management, but don't think manufactures make it easy for you. For example, two pastries may come in one package, but the label says one serving is 200 calories—for "one pastry".

Calories and Calories from Fat—This tells you how many calories are in one serving and how many of those calories come from fat.

Nutrients by Weight and Percentage of Daily Value (%DV)—This shows how much of each nutrient is in one serving by weight in grams and by %DV. This symbol refers to the recommended daily allowance for a nutrient based on a 2,000-calorie diet. (Note, some nutrients like sugar and protein don't have a %DV.) Fats are listed as "total fat" and also broken down so you can see how much is unhealthy saturated fat and trans fat.

Vitamins and Minerals—Vitamins and minerals are listed by %DV only. Pay particular attention to Vitamin A, Vitamin C, Calcium, and Iron; most Americans don't get enough of those in their diets.

Ingredients—Listed in order from the greatest amount to the least.

REMEMBER—The fewer the ingredients, the better the product!

Shop With Stacy

FILL YOUR FREEZER:

Ground beef

Chicken breasts

Frozen berries

Frozen veggies—store-bought or, better yet, pre-cooked by you!

Frozen seasonings—onions, peppers, stir-fry type veggies

Shrimp

Frozen fish—cod or tilapia

Ezekiel bread

RESTOCK YOUR REFRIGERATOR:

Salsas

Condiments— lemon and lime juice, balsamic vinegar, red wine vinegar, mustard, and low-sugar ketchup

Tomatoes, cucumber, salad mix

Cottage cheese (organic only)

All other veggies that will be quickly consumed

Pack Your Pantry:

Whole-wheat pasta, brown rice penne pasta

Beans—canned black or cannellini

Broth

Pasta sauce—no sugar added

Brown rice

Balsamic vinegar

Oatmeal (plain oats)

Rice cakes

Cream of rice

Raw almonds

Meal Mapping

You have your shopping list—now let's dive deeper into your meal mapping.

Macro recap:

Protein

Remember, protein = power!

This power macro burns calories.

Daily dose = Three to four ounces at a time, at least five times a day. Yes, I said five times per day!

Why you need it: Keep your metabolism going, slow down the glycemic effect of carbs and fats, and sustain your lean body mass.

Carbs

Carbs = your main energy fuel source.

WARNING: Eat too much, and it will be stored as body fat!

Daily dose= Limit this to four ounces, twice a day (this will change as we progress). NO processed carbohydrates or sugar.

Fruits & Veggies

Go green!

Green veggies are full of water-packed molecules but don't a play role in affecting blood sugar levels.

Stay away from high-sugar fruits such as bananas, oranges, and pineapples this month. I would also recommend staying away from carrots, corn, and peas. They offer little nutritional value and are full of sugar.

Fat

Cut the fat to one time a day.

Remember this is the highest calorie-per-gram macronutrient... but you need it for bride-beautiful hair, skin, and nails.

Watch the saturated fats that come from cheeses and fatty animal proteins. These are high in cholesterol and saturated fat.

Recap:

Remember, it's not just what you eat, but how much of it you eat.

This month, limit your proteins and carbohydrates to 3 to 4 ounces per meal, five times a day. Make sure your starchy carbs are limited to two times a day and no more than 4 ounces (or half a cup) at a time. Fats are limited to one time a day and 2 ounces per serving.

Now that you know quantity, let's review quality.

QUALITY PROTEIN

My top-quality protein picks are: chicken, egg whites, tilapia, cod or any other lean white fish, lean ground turkey, or lean ground beef or sirloin.

Bridal blunders when it comes to picking protein:

1. Don't be a wiener!

Toss the deli meats full of nitrates, preservatives, sodium, and sugars. They have little to no nutritional value and offer no real protein content.

2. Don't be a dairy queen!

This is always a hot topic for me. People think dairy is a high-quality protein source, and it can be, if it's organic and coming from a good source. But typically people use non-organic milk products that are filled with hormones, pesticides, and antibiotics. It can also cause the mucous membrane to inflame and cause a mucus buildup. Gross!

3. Skip the bars.

We're not talking booze, although by now you should know there's no alcohol allowed, either. We are talking about something that seems so much more innocent—the protein bar. These are usually high-calorie, high-fat, and high-sugar, and they have very little quality protein involved. They are man-made and usually highly processed, making this a diet no-no.

QUALITY CARBS

By now you should have cleaned out the processed carbohydrates from your cabinet. Quick, get rid of the boxes, bags, and bars! They are high in sugar and preservatives, and offer no quality nutrition.

My top-five quality carbs are: rice of any kind or color, potatoes of any kind or color, plain oatmeal, plain rice cakes, or Ezekiel bread.

Bridal blunders when it comes to choosing carbs:

1. Counting Carrots

Stick to 18 carats when it comes to your gold, but when it comes to your diet, consider skipping carrots altogether.

We tend to grab a bag of carrots, thinking we are choosing a healthy veggie as a snack—but we also tend to overindulge and eat the whole bag. This leads to over 200 calories, consisting of carbs and sugars.

So unless you're only going to have 10 to 15, stay away.

2. The hundred-calorie snack pack.

These make me crazy. Yes, it's true that there are only 100 calories. However, these snack pack bags are usually full of highly processed carbohydrates, sugars, and preservatives which offer no quality nutrition. Instead, they spike blood sugar and leave you with a crashing effect—making you want more sugar and carbs!

3. The pretzel.

The worst offender and almost always a top pick. All low-calorie pretzels are made from white flour and are very high in carbohydrates. Pretzels offer a very low nutritional value, high glycemic index, and no protein at all. It's another snack that we usually overindulge in, and can lead to 300 to 400 empty calories packed with carbs that our bodies won't utilize.

Quality Fats

I'll say it again: Stay away from saturated fats and fats that are found in animal proteins and cheeses. These fats are high in cholesterol and sodium, and offer very little nutritional value. When eating fats, choose fats from good natural sources that offer you omega-3s, -6s, and -9s.

My top-five fat picks are: avocado, salmon, olive oil, flax, and natural organic almonds and peanut butters.

Bridal blunders when it comes to trimming the fat:

1. Don't go nuts with nuts!

Portions, my friends. This is one case where a 100-calorie snack pack is good, because it will limit your portions. Don't tempt yourself by buying a big bag—it can lead to consuming 500 to 600 calories at a time. Ah nuts!

2. Going down the wrong path with trail mix.

Unless you have the willpower of Gandhi, don't buy trail mix as a snack. Again, usually offering nuts and dried fruit and sometimes chocolate or yogurt, this snack is very high in calories, fat, and sugar, and is usually very highly preserved, packed with chemicals. It raises your blood sugar and makes you crave—you guessed it—more carbs, fats, and sugars. And, if you eat half of a cup, you can consume over 650 calories. So stay far away, or unhappy trails to you.

3. Olive oil spoil.

Pile on Popeye's spinach—but only use small sprays of olive oil!

Too much of a good thing can be bad. Olive oil is 16g of fat per tablespoon. Typically it is *poured* on our salads and vegetables, yielding over 500 calories and fats that we can't utilize.

4. Who moved my cheese?

It was me. Stay away from the cheese—in salads or cheese snack sticks, it's everywhere and full of hormones, preservatives, and antibiotics. Cheese will never help you lose weight.

Got it? So, now you know what to eat. What should you wash it all down with? WATER!

How much water?

64 ounces a day is a minimum. If you're exercising, and you should be exercising, you must drink at least 72 ounces, or a gallon a day.

Remember, our bodies are 60 percent water, and we need to replenish that water for energy and proper health! Brides, you need both!

Maybe this will encourage you to fill that bottle: Not drinking enough water can cause fatigue (and you don't have time to be tired!), allergic reactions (yuk), high blood pressure (dangerous), and nasty skin issues (there goes that blushing bride glow).

NOT-SO-FUN FACT: Dehydration impairs the elimination of toxins from the skin, making you more vulnerable to skin problems like psoriasis, acne, wrinkling, discoloration, and black lace around the eyes. Not pretty for pictures!

Let's talk water and weight loss. When your cells are depleted of water, and therefore energy, we tend to eat more—but we are really just thirsty!

Plus, you can't properly digest without enough water and alkaline minerals (like calcium and magnesium). If you are not drinking enough water, it can lead to many digestive issues, including gas, bloating, and irregular bowels—making it nearly impossible to lose weight. So stop the drought, and drink up!

VITAMINS

There are so many on the market. Here's the thing: We excrete at least 60 percent of the vitamins that we are taking in, only making 30 percent of the actual vitamin content usable.

Don't overindulge in vitamins—it can actually be toxic to your internal organs.

So here's what you need:

Emergen-C or pure vitamin C

Take 1,000 milligrams. This will provide anti-inflammatory agents to help keep you looking your best and will also aid in immunity, a great aid in keeping you healthy during this most stressful time of your life.

Biotin

I love biotin! It regulates blood sugar, helps with the prevention of hair loss, and even strengthens your fingernails and your hair follicles. How's that for bridal beauty?!

B complex

B complex includes B12, B6, and B3, making this the best energy-boosting vitamin. Here's a B-bonus: It also has stress-relieving factors and can boost your metabolism by helping relax the adrenals.

EATING ORGANIC

Organic food should be locally grown, with no pesticides, no hormones, and no antibiotics used. This is very important when choosing lean meat, chicken, pork, and dairy products, including eggs.

SO WHERE DO I SHOP FOR ALL OF THIS?

All of us, at least here on the East Coast, know of Whole Foods, Trader Joe's, the regular supermarkets, etc. etc. etc.

If you are familiar with Whole Foods, you know they offer high-quality proteins, vegetables, and meats, as well as a full-blown vitamin shop.

Trader Joe's is a specialty supermarket, and could be a less expensive option. Just note that they are not all organic. I shop Trader Joe's for Ezekial Bread and my favorite, a good coconut oil spray.

And when all else fails, check your local supermarket. I frequent Stop & Shop, as they are well priced and provide high-quality produce meats and even have their own organic brand called Nature's Promise. You can sometimes find Ezekial Bread in their freezer section as well.

Elisa's Survival Tips

IF YOU WANT SOMETHING YOU'VE NEVER HAD, YOU'VE GOT TO DO
SOMETHING YOU'VE NEVER DONE.

1ST STEP-PREP!

The key to my success was preparation. I leave the house for work at 3:00 a.m., and with my jam-packed schedule and long days, I have very little time to cook. I learned that I had to make food prep a priority and incorporate it into my schedule. On Sundays, I do my shopping and cook ahead for the week. I make sure I have my food already weighed out and packed in individual servings in the fridge so I can grab and go. I found it is much easier if you prepare your food in bulk.

PACK SNACKS!

I made sure (and still make sure!) I always had my packed prepared snacks with me to avoid any temptation to grab something not on my Bridal Body plan. As much as all of the preparation is time-consuming, it actually reduced the stress in my life. I never had to worry about what—or when—I was going to eat. In the long run, it has saved me time, calories, and money, although my local deliverymen and women miss me!

TEA FOR ME

I do a lot of networking. Instead of going to lunches, I meet business colleagues and even friends for tea. You'll be surprised how much more gets accomplished during teatime! Warning—be sure to avoid the biscuits!

DINNER DATES

My social life did suffer a little bit. I had to reduce my dinner dates, which ended up being okay because I had a lot of wedding planning to do! It also resulted in me spending more quality time (and less money) with my fiancé.

When you do go out to dinner, do not arrive hungry. I made sure I ate beforehand, and then ordered something very light and healthy. Remember to order something steamed or grilled with no extra oil. My fiancé and I always asked to skip the breadbasket to take away the temptation on the table!

BUZZKILL

There's no way around it: If you want the Bridal Body, you have to eliminate the alcohol. Buzzkill, I know. If you must have a drink, and there will be nights during wedding planning (just wait 'til you have to do table arrangements) that you must—choose wisely, and have Stacy's red wine spritzer! (See pg. 132 for recipe) I am proud to say that I am now a much cheaper date.

Stacy's Weekly Plan Prep

Designate at least one meal plan prep day. Sunday works best for me. Pre-cook all of your meat, some of your starches, and your veggies.

STACY SUGGESTS: Buy in bulk! To save money, find a butcher shop in your neighborhood. They sell meat in bulk! Separate it into servings, cook some now, and freeze the rest. Be sure to date the frozen chicken and cook within two to three weeks, if you have a regular freezer. If you have a deep freezer, you may freeze it for up to two months.

Marinate meats in different seasonings so you don't get bored. Cook it. Break out that food scale and split meat into servings. Separate those servings into containers.

STACY SUGGESTS: Go Cold Turkey! Make a hotel-style turkey in the oven for the week. If you like turkey sandwiches and miss deli meat, try this. A hotel-style turkey is a real turkey minus the wings and legs. It cooks in about one hour instead of three! When the turkey is cooked and still hot, slice it up! Freeze half for next week's meals, and leave the rest in the fridge.

Next, cook a pot of brown rice. You can add chicken broth to the water to spice it up. While you are doing that, take however many sweet potatoes you want for the week and wrap them in tin foil. Put them in the oven on 350 for 40-60 minutes. Note: Cooking them slowly makes them caramelize. Weigh out your starch servings and add them to your cooked and weighed protein containers.

Last, prepare your veggies. It's up to you if you want to cook them ahead. If you do, par boil or steam them so when you reheat them, they still have some crunch. Then add to your containers.

STACY SUGGESTS: Go Green! Green veggies are nutrient-packed. I grow them in my garden every year. I love to prepare them with smoked turkey so they have lots of flavor. Buy smoked turkey legs from the meat section of the supermarket already cooked. Boil them in a Dutch oven (big pot) filled halfway with water. After 15 minutes of boiling, drop in your greens (try collards first) already chopped into small strips. Turn the heat down and boil them for another half hour. This will make lots of greens! If you want to eat the turkey, leave it in the water when you add your greens. By the time it is done cooking, the meat will fall right off the bone—yum!

By Wednesday, you might have to revisit the grocery story for perishables. Otherwise, you should be good to go!

Travel Tips

*I*f you travel, make your menu in advance. Cook everything and portion it into re-sealable storage bags labeled with the day and what meal it is. Pack in a cooler bag with ice packs. Call ahead to your hotel and request to have a fridge in your room.

HERE'S WHAT TO PACK.

Oatmeal: Most hotels have microwaves. Bring empty microwave friendly containers with you. You will use it to prepare your oatmeal. Use the coffee machine in your room to boil the water, but be sure to wash the machine thoroughly by running water and vinegar/lemon (bring it with you too!) through it—this will get rid of the coffee taste in the machine.

Nothing is nastier than coffee oatmeal! Yuk!

If there is no coffee pot available, just add hot water to your oatmeal and mix thoroughly.

Also bring: chicken, turkey, Ezekiel bread, brown rice cakes for post-workout, lots of broccoli (keep raw so it doesn't get mushy) and asparagus, apples, nuts, and a few scoops of whey protein. Plus don't forget a can opener. When you reach your destination, you can shop for egg whites, a container of strawberries, and organic cottage cheese. Never pack dairy for your trip, buy it when you get there so it doesn't spoil!

Buy mini containers that hold a tablespoon's worth of condiments—so great for salsa, mustard, etc., and so much easier than bringing along the whole jar!

Remember, you must pre-measure and arrange your meals before you go.

Part Three

LET'S GET MOVIN'

Don't wish for it. Work for it.

No Gym or Trainer Necessary!

Let's be honest. How much exercise are you getting? First things first: Add 20 minutes to what you are already doing, and do it three days a week. You should be doing both weight training and cardiovascular exercise. If your goal is weight loss, ramp up your cardio. If it's toning, increase your weight training by sets, reps, or both! No gym membership? No problem. Get a jump rope for high-intensity training intervals.

The heart of the matter: It's quality over quantity when it comes to exercising.

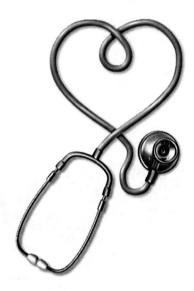

Target heart rate zone—To lose weight and utilize fat loss, you must keep your heart in the target heart rate zone. So what is your target heart rate zone?

There are different levels of intensity:

1. Low zone, 50 percent of max heart rate

2. Target zone, 65 percent of max heart rate

3. Cardio zone or HIT ZONE, 75/80 percent of max heart rate

4. Max heart rate, 90-100 percent of max heart rate

Let's do the math.

Heart Rate Equation:

220 minus your age equals _____

Take that number and multiply it by the heart rate zone that you're looking to achieve. That is the heart rate, or beats per minute, that you should be in.

For example: My age is 36.

220 - 36 = 184

184 x .65 = 120 BPM, and that number equals the target heart rate zone. To burn fat, you need to be in that zone. The HIT zone, or cardio zone, has its benefits as well, helping with performance. The low zone will burn calories.

Set the Timer

To burn the optimal amount of body fat, you must be in the target heart rate zone for more than 30 minutes at a time, but no more than 60 to 70 minutes, or you run the risk of running into lean body mass stores, which you do not want to use to fuel your trainings.

> **TRAINING TIP:** Purchase a great heart rate monitor to keep track of your heart rate, or you could be wasting your time—and brides-to-be don't have time to waste!

Sometimes less is more, but before I met Stacy, I never thought that way in terms of workouts. I dreaded getting on the treadmill. I would go as fast as I could, for as long as I could, burning as many calories as I could. I was winded, exhausted, and pretty miserable. When Stacy taught me about my target heart rate zone, my treadmill time actually became enjoyable. I work up a sweat but feel good doing my 45 minutes of a brisk walk while I listen to my playlist or catch up on some TV. Lesson:

WORK HARD AND SMART!

No goal was ever met... Without a little sweat.

Cardio Goal:

Weeks 1 & 2—Our goal is to perform 20-30 minutes of fat-burning cardio. Remember, you must utilize your heart rate zone (page 62 if you skipped it).

You will do this at least twice—ideally three days a week.

You can use any machine at the gym—elliptical, treadmill, stairs—bride's choice. Or simply walk briskly outside.

Use your heart rate monitor to be sure you are burning fat calories.

Weeks 3 & 4—Add 10 minutes to your fat-burning sessions—and make the three days a week mandatory!

Pump That Iron—Don't be scared of bulk

Be excited to get strong with strength training and toning exercises to shape your muscles and your body.

But let's face a few facts first. To gain muscle mass, you must have an excess of 2,500 calories in your diet in order to put on one pound of lean body mass. Most women do not allow themselves to eat even the necessary amount of calories to sustain lean body mass, never mind eating 2,500 calories *more*. You also need to be resistance training in a range of 6 to 10 reps using enough weight to reproduce lean muscle cells. This type of protocol needs to happen for a long period of time in order to gain the amount of lean body mass that women are afraid of putting on.

As women, we lose 1 percent of lean body mass per year after the age of 35. But, unfortunately, this does not work in weight loss. Muscle tissue is the only tissue on our body that is metabolic—that will help us burn calories without doing anything. *So remember, the more lean body mass you own, the more calories you will burn.* Training with light weights at reasonable repetitions will increase muscle cells, but not at the rate that builds bulk. These exercises will burn calories, plus the resulting muscle tissue will help us burn calories, so it's a double win!

TONE IT UP

All brides can use toning. Wake up those muscles that haven't been working in a while!

This training is quick, simple, and can be done at home. It's also highly effective for working all of your major muscle groups and your core, and it is safe for all levels.

YOU NEED: A pair of 5-pound dumbbells.

Main Goal: Weight Loss

Workout Type: WORKOUT A - Stacy's Foundation Training

Level: Beginner

Equipment: Dumbbells and a mat

WEEK'S WORKOUT

MONDAY	TUESDAY	WEDNESDAY	THURSDAY	FRIDAY	SATURDAY	SUNDAY
Cardio	Weight Training	Cardio	Weight Training	Cardio	Cardio	Rest!

HERE'S THE BREAKDOWN

Weeks 1-2

- Do two sets of all of the exercises below, 12 reps per exercise.
- Rest 30-45 seconds between each set
- Do not move on to the next exercise until you have completed all sets and reps

1. Pushup—Full or on your knees

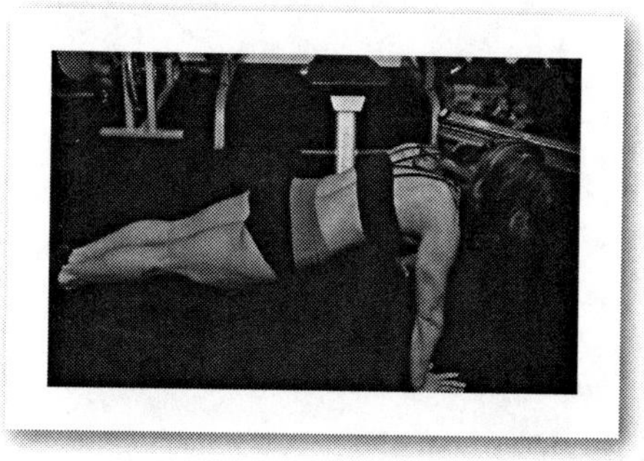

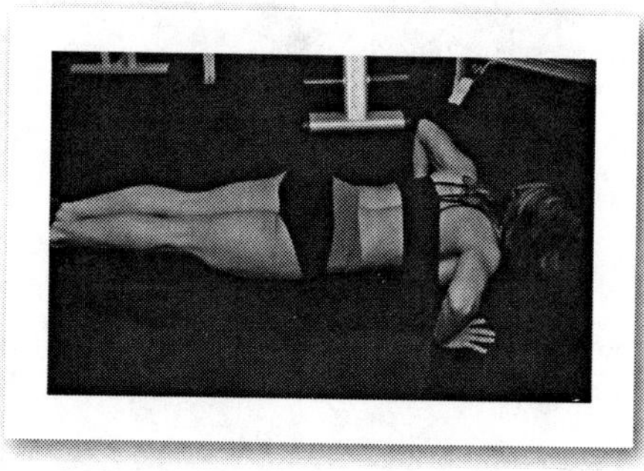

2. Plank—Hold until muscule failure occurs

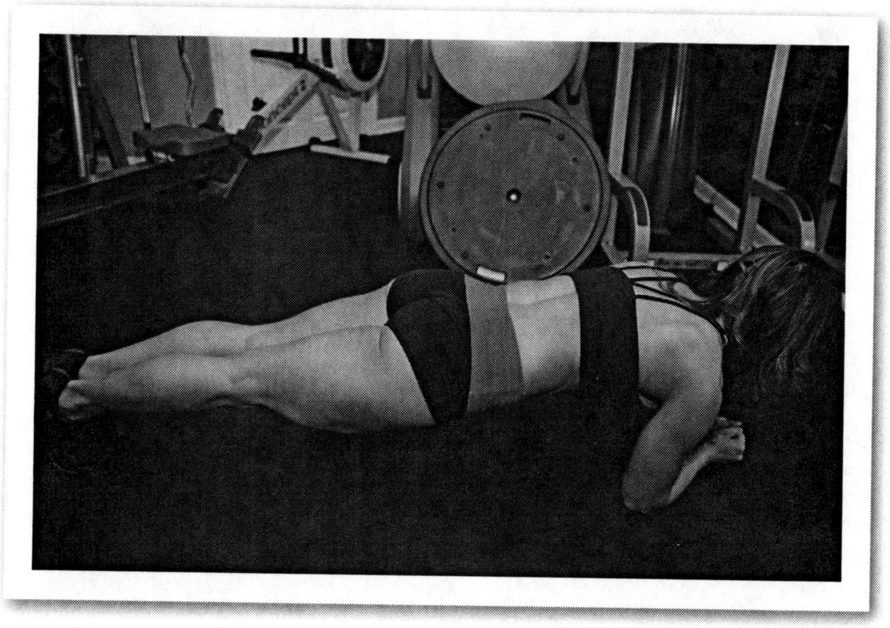

3. Squat—90°, if you can

4. Crunches or hanging chair raise

5. Military dumbbell press—Seated on a chair or bench

 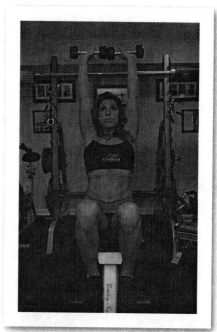

6. Reverse lunges—Alternating

7. Assisted pull-up —If in the gym; otherwise, we will perform a standing one-arm dumbbell row

8. Standing toe raises

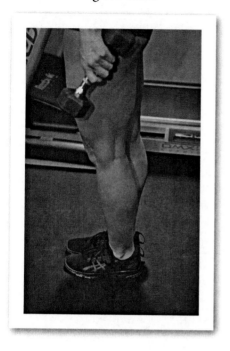 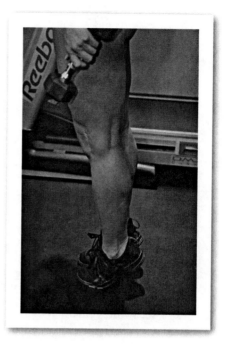

PLEASE VISIT BRIDALBODYBOOK.COM FOR HOW-TO EXERCISE VIDEO TUTORIALS.

I DON'T FIND THE TIME TO EXERCISE, I MAKE THE TIME TO EXERCISE.

Part Four

A GOAL WITHOUT A PLAN IS JUST A WISH.

My Goal Pyramid

Let's set some goals!

SET YOUR LONG-TERM GOALS

Example of Elisa's Long-Term Goals: Lose 20 pounds, reduce body fat by 8-10 percent, tone arms and back, tone tummy, drop two dress sizes

_____

_____

_____

SET YOUR MONTHLY GOALS

Example of Elisa's Monthly Goals: Drop 8 lbs, lose 2 percent BF, lose an inch off each arm

_____

_____

_____

SET YOUR WEEKLY GOALS

Example of Elisa's Weekly Goals: Lose 2 lbs, get two workouts in, grocery shop, and prep meals

_____

_____

_____

SET YOUR DAILY GOALS

Break your week up and get things accomplished

Example of Elisa's Daily Goals

Monday: Cardio, document food intake (journal)

Tuesday: Weight training and grocery shop, journal

Wednesday: Cook for end of week and weekend

Thursday: Weight training and journal

Friday: Cardio, other wedding tasks, and journal

Saturday: Reward meal or reward massage or facial, journal and rest!

Sunday: Cardio, wedding tasks, family time, grocery shop, and prepare for the week ahead.

* If program is changing, make a new grocery list

Monday: _____

Tuesday: _____

Wednsday: _____

Thursday: _____

Friday:_____

Saturday: _____

Sunday: _____

Just a few Bridal Body reminders:

Eat every three hours—Remember, we want to create metabolic stimulation and stabilize blood sugar, so make sure you don't skip meals!

Lose Fake Foods—We hope you've processed this! Processed foods raise blood sugar and offer little to no nutritional value—so lose them.

Buy a food scale and learn how to measure—Portion control is half the battle. All food will be measured *after* cooking.

Don't Weigh in Daily—This can really dampen your mood if you don't lose every day or see the scale drop. Remember it's a journey and will take time. Different things can cause weight not to change from day to day, so don't get down if you don't see daily changes.

AT FIRST THEY'LL ASK YOU WHY YOU ARE DOING IT.

LATER THEY'LL ASK YOU HOW YOU DID IT.

Find Support—Get with people who are on the same mission or want you to be successful. Nobody needs a Debbie Downer when preparing for your big day.

Ditch the Haters—Girls, let's face it: Sometimes friends are jealous, and these so-called friends don't want us to succeed. Watch out for saboteurs and get rid of them.

WHEN YOU FEEL LIKE QUITTING, THINK ABOUT WHY YOU STARTED.

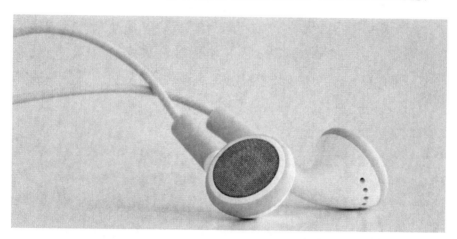

If You Need Some Workout Inspiration, Here's Stacy's All-Time Favorites To Add To Your Workout Playlist!

I'm So Excited – Pointer Sisters

Jump – Pointer Sisters

Eye of the Tiger – Survivor

Welcome to the Jungle – Guns N' Roses

Strike It Up – Black Box

Up in Here – DMX

Paper Cut – Linkin Park

Four Minutes – Justin Timberlake & Madonna

Kick-Start My Heart – Motley Crue

Holding Out for Hero – Bonnie Tyler

Footloose – Kenny Loggins

I Wanna Dance with Somebody – Whitney Houston

Into the Groove – Madonna

Nothing's Gonna Stop Us Now – Starship

It's Raining Men – Gloria Gaynor

Hot Stuff – Donna Summer

Let's Go Crazy – Prince

Here's Music That Gets Elisa Moving:

Chapel of Love – Bette Midler

Walking on Sunshine – Katrina & The Waves

Shake It – Metro Station

Dance Again – Jennifer Lopez (featuring Pitbull)

Raise Your Glass – Pink

Club Can't Handle Me – Flo Rida (featuring David Guetta)

Bulletproof – La Roux

Give Me Everything – Pitbull (featuring Ne-Yo, AfroJack)

Work B***ch – Britney Spears

Jump – Van Halen

Jump Around – House of Pain

Night Still Young – Nicki Minaj

I Love It – Icono Pop (featuring Charli XCX)

Time of Our Lives – Pitbull, Ne-Yo

Roar – Katy Perry

Fight Song- Rachel Platten

More playlists to follow!

THE COUNTDOWN BEGINS....

Ladies, by now you should be seeing some major changes in your Bridal Body.

Let's track your progress on The Bridal Body worksheet on page 121 and be honest, so that you can be accountable.

So, we are two to three months away from the big day. We need to get even more serious now and really attack the goals that we set.

If you think you are busy now, just wait and hold on tight. I don't mean to stress you out even more. I do mean to motivate you to reach your goals now before you have even more to do. And trust me, you will have more to do. Two and a half months before my wedding I hit the 20-pound loss. All of a sudden I saw a major change in my body, and everyone around me started noticing. I felt major relief, major pride, and major motivation to keep going. For the first time in a long time, I

This is prime planning time. Your stress level is high, your to-do list is long, and your free minutes are few and far between. We get it.

So take a deep breath, and let's focus.

Here's what you need to do:

1. Meal Prepping

This is mandatory now. No missing meals. No cheating.

Maybe find a buddy, or ask your future hubby to help.

Pick a day and time, and make those meals!

Remember: Not planned or prepared, then prepare to fail.

Be sure to have brown rice cakes, almonds, carrots, and grilled chicken strips with you when you travel, in case you're on the road and get stuck somewhere.

2. Stay hydrated

Water must be a big part of your day. Staying hydrated will keep you full, keep your skin looking beautiful, and also help rev up that metabolism since it aids digestion and the entire metabolic system. At this point, one gallon is the goal.

H2-oh-no. I had such a hard time getting in my gallon of water. Here's how I did it: I drank an entire bottle of water when I woke up. I sipped hot water with my breakfast. And all day I carried around a gallon-sized reusable bottle that Stacy gave me so I could track how much more I needed to drink. I had my goal and could see my progress. I traveled with Emergen-C and fresh cut lemons just in case I needed a little flavor. After a few weeks, and lots of trips to the restroom, I saw a huge difference in my skin and overall wellbeing. I'll drink to that!

3. Keep calm, and use stress reduction techniques!

It's totally normal to have a lot of stress right now, but it's how you control and handle that stress that matters. Don't let cortisol affect your weight loss! Cortisol is a hormone in the body secreted by the adrenal glands. It regulates blood sugar, aids in glucose metabolism, and helps with immunity and inflammatory responses. When your cortisol level is elevated, your body is telling you it's under too much stress. When your body is tired and in "fight or flight" mode, your weight will increase due to inflammation. It will also slow down all metabolic processes, including fat and glucose metabolism. So yes, stress can make you fat. So... don't stress, and use my techniques below to help you.

I remember this so clearly. It was a little less than two months until the big day. I was flipping channels and the end of the movie Bridesmaids *was on. Lillian turned to Annie and said, "Wasn't it my turn to be crazy? The bride's supposed to be crazy, right?" Boy, could I relate (and in a weird way it made me feel better)! I felt crazy. I was constantly crying (and I am not a crier)—every time I heard a sad-ish song on the radio, every time I thought of all the things I still had to do, and every time I thought about the wedding being over. Crazy. I was totally overwhelmed with emotion and totally stressed out. The best thing I did was start taking out time for me. I wish I had done it sooner. Besides my gym time (which became therapeutic), I started scheduling facials and massages. I took out some time to spend with my girlfriends. Mo (my groom) and I started taking dance lessons (that brought out a lot of laughs) and planned some no-wedding-talk nights out and even a weekend getaway. I vowed to do one "fun" thing every day before my wedding—and I did. Friends and strangers alike kept telling me to enjoy this time, that it's the best time of my life, to soak in all of the love and have fun. It was, and I am so happy I did. I hope you do too.*

Having fun at dance lessons with our instructor Martin Rebello at Arthur Murray in Plainview, Long Island

Stacy's Stress Suppressants:

1. Schedule a massage

A deep-tissue massage can help stressed muscles. Aromatherapy can also be added for extra relaxation.

2. Drink chamomile tea

Chamomile has a calming effect on the body and tastes yummy. (***Elisa's Bridal Body beauty bonus***—put your tea bag in the freezer and use to de-puff your under-eyes!)

3. Do yoga

It's true! Yoga will loosen tight muscle tissue. It also relaxes the brain and the body from our everyday stress and allows the mind to clear.

4. Read something other than bridal magazines (and your to-do list)!

This needs no explanation!

5. Walk your dog!

We're not trading in our engagement rings, but whoever said diamonds are a girl's best friend never had a dog—or a cat! An animal is proven to reduce stress and have a calming effect on the central nervous system. If you don't have a pet, local shelters are always looking for helping hands to volunteer!

6. Take your groom to his room

Some intimate time with your mate, not focusing on wedding plans but rather on each other, will lead to intimacy and help you calm down and relax. It will also promote bonding that might not have taken place during these last couple of months.

7. Laugh

Go see a comedy show or watch a funny movie. Laughing is proven to decrease stress levels by 50 percent.

8. Dance

Going out for a dance can be fun (heck, it even burns calories), but stay away from the drinks, and don't stay out too late!

9. Don't wait until your honeymoon to get away!

Get away, even if it's just for the day. Give yourself a break. A change of atmosphere can be great for the mind and soul.

10. Sleep

When we don't sleep, we don't recover, and we don't recoup from all of the stress. Our bodies cannot handle any fewer than six hours per night, especially when you're wedding planning and achieving The Bridal Body.

One of the best things I did during the wedding planning process was go on a girls' getaway. Three months before my wedding, my best friend from college planned a trip to Mexico to her timeshare and convinced me to go! I didn't want to spend the money, I was worried about all I had to do, and, of course, I worried about my workouts! But going was one of the best pre-wedding decisions I made. We had so many laughs. I brought my wedding magazines, and my friends were so happy to help me pull some ideas—poolside. I vented and released so much stress I didn't even know that I had built up. I slept in. We all went to the spa for massages. I worked out in the gym and did my cardio on the beach, which was so much more fun to do with friends! And I brought along my snacks and oatmeal packets (see page 59 for Bridal Body travel tips!), and had meals made to order—and, believe it or not, lost weight along the way! I came home rested and excited to continue planning, and missing my fiancé!

Okay, back to work!

It's time to up your exercise—and add intensity!

Better sore than sorry.

Main Goal: Increase Lean Body Mass and Fat Loss

Workout Type: WORKOUT B- Interval Training

Training Level: Moderate

Days per Week: 3-4

Equipment: Jump Rope, Kettlebell, Pair of Heavier Dumbbells

WEEK'S WORKOUT

MONDAY	TUESDAY	WEDNESDAY	THURSDAY	FRIDAY	SATURDAY	SUNDAY
Training & Cardio	Cardio	Rest	Training	Training & Cardio	Training & Cardio	Rest!

THE TWO-WEEK PLAN:

1. Add in intervals to your training

2. Increase your training days to 4-6 times a week.

*Just by adding an additional two days of calorie-/fat-burning training, you will now increase fat loss and shed more pounds quickly—and that clock is ticking!

So what does "Add Intensity" mean?

The training time will be cut down, since we are now doing more at once.

You can add intensity by:

❧ Adding reps/sets

❧ Decreasing rest periods or have no rest periods

❧ Adding in fat-burning cardio between sets

Oh, and there's more… We will also be adding in additional toning exercises to help target special areas. Let's go; challenge yourself. You can do this!

In case you need convincing…

The Benefits of Interval Training and High-Intensity Interval Training (HIIT):

1. Time-saving

2. Increase fat burning—to lose weight, not muscle

3. Increase lung capacity and can decrease high blood pressure

4. Increase metabolism

Plus, there's no gym required—just some simple supplies. You don't need the following to succeed, but they help:

1. An additional pair of dumbbells

2. A jump rope

3. A kettlebell, 15 lb.

4. A good mat, especially if you are rug-less with hard floors.

Jump Rope for Stacy!

Jumping rope is one of Stacy's favorite cardio choices. It burns tons of calories, keeping the heart rate elevated—and it's lots of fun. Double dutch if you dare!

Cha-Cha-Cha Changes

Do you see your body changing? Good! As we change our training, and as your body changes, our dietary intake must change. As we lose weight, we need less food to keep us going. We will need more protein for recovery and proper fuel, but we are now aiming to spend more calories in the gym and eat less of the energy macros that get stored as fat if unused.

Goal: Add exercises, intensify trainings, maximize time, reduce calories, lose pounds.

So, let's add in new exercises.

Go to BridalBodyBook.com for video tutorials.

1. Standing Dumbbell Lateral Raises

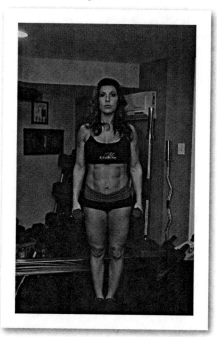 

2. Standing Bicep Hammer Curls

3. Tricep Dumbbell Kickbacks

4. V Ups

5. Plank to Push Up

6. Walking Lunges

7. Glute Bridges

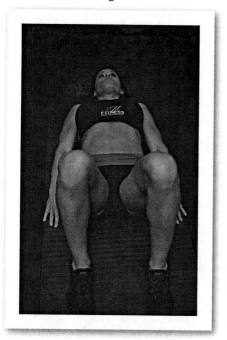 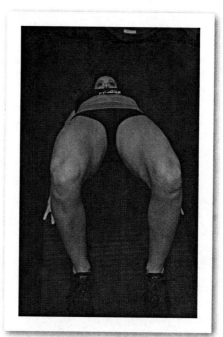

8. Stiff Dead Legged Dead Lifts

9. Jump Rope

10. Kettlebell Swings

CARDIO WORKOUT

Training:

You were doing 20-30 minutes of your fat-burning cardio three days a week.

Add ten minutes more and train four days a week to maximize fat loss and increase calorie spending.

STACY'S TRAINING TIP:

For bigger results quicker, do this on a fasted empty stomach in order to utilize fat storage faster.

If not, we can do this in the evening after a weight-training interval session. Remember, this cardio is still in a target heart rate, cardio fat-burning zone.

As far as our high-intensity intervals, they should be done at least two to three times a week— on top of the fat burning cardio sessions.

If, and only if, you cannot do both, I would prefer that you do the interval. Please do not neglect the fat-burning cardio, but if it's one or the other, it has to be the interval. Because your body is not used to this type of training, it will automatically increase calorie spending and use fat storage faster.

♥ **Heart Rate Zone:** This is going to be in a different heart rate zone. It will normally bring your heart rate to 65 or 75 percent of your maximum heart rate.

Don't forget to do the math.

220 (-) your age (x) .75 = your cardio high-intensity zone.

Do not to stay in the zone for more than 25 to 30 minutes. This will cause lean body mass to start fueling the training, which we do not want. Our goal is to lose fat, not muscle.

STRENGTH TRAINING

Warm it up!

For five minutes, run in place, walk briskly, or bicycle to get the blood flowing!

Training time!

For the next 20-30 minutes, interval the weight training exercises and add in the cardio directly after weight training. There's no rest between sets! Once you complete the first round, you will rest for one minute.

Repeat it twice and continue through these exercises until complete.

I chose this panel of exercises because they focus on the major muscle groups that stand out in a wedding dress: sexy shoulders, toned arms, tight tummy, sculpted legs, beautiful butt. Sound good? Follow this regimen perfectly, and you will hit all of your desired areas, burn maximal amounts of fat, and look your bridal best on your big day.

READY, SET, BRIDAL BURN!

* 12-15 reps per exercise, and 2-3 sets

Standing Dumbbell Lateral Raises

Standing Dumbbell Hammer Curls

Run in Place 60 seconds

Tricep Dumbbell Kick Back

Crunches on Floor

60 Second Jump Rope

Walking Lunges

Glutes Bridges

60 Second Kettle Swing

Stiff Leg Dead Lift

Plank to Push Up

Run in Place 60 Seconds

V Ups

Jumping Jacks 60 Seconds

Keep going! If you have time after you complete this workout, continue with your fat-burning cardio.

By doing your slow and steady cardio after high intensity, you are bound to tap into stubborn, stored body fat. To effectively and efficiently maximize results, do the cardio directly after your high-intensity training.

Don't forget to turn to page 121 and track your progress on The Bridal Body worksheet.

ELISA'S PLAYLIST:

Break My Stride – Matthew Wilder

Across the Clouds – Amber

It's My Life – Bon Jovi

Run the World – Beyoncé

Lose Control – Missy Elliot (featuring Fatman Scoop & Ciara)

Conga – Gloria Estefan

On the Floor – Jennifer Lopez

American Boy – Estelle (featuring Kanye West)

Tricky – RUN-DMC

Let's Go – Calvin Harris (featuring Ne-Yo)

Stronger – Kelly Clarkson

Fighter – Christina Aguilera

Not Afraid – Eminem

Bang Bang – Jessie J, Ariana Grande, & Nicki Minaj

We're Not Gonna Take It – Twisted Sister

One Way or Another – Blondie

Girl on Fire – Alicia Keys

E As if you have any time to schedule any additional appointments... I know. In addition to Stacy's recommended massages, here are some others you should consider:

Spray Tan: If you are thinking of adding an extra glow, consider a DHA-based sunless tanner. I got married at the end of summer, so even though I stayed out of the sun, I ended up with good color. I didn't end up getting sprayed for my big day, but I do get a spray tan for every other special event. A good spray professional can add even more definition to your Bridal Body! But make sure you test it out first (my friend was allergic!) and get to know and trust the professional well in advance of the wedding day spray! (And don't go too dark—you want to look like the best version of YOU!)

Dermatologist: Between my change in diet, workouts, and stress, my skin needed help! Don't wait until the week before your wedding. Several months in advance, see your dermatologist. My dermatologist recommended special skincare products and put me on a schedule for DermaSweep facials. My skin never looked better than it did on my wedding day. I was truly glowing.

Dentist: You should have so much to smile about! Flash those pearly—clean—whites! Call your dentist and schedule a cleaning. I used whitening strips to freshen up my teeth the week before the wedding. (Again, test well in advance first; you don't want sensitivity.) And don't floss right before the wedding—you don't want swollen gums in your photos!

WILLPOWER IS A MUSCLE.
THE MORE YOU USE IT, THE STRONGER IT GETS.

Final Countdown

We are almost there, and you got this!

Let's break it down. Here's where we are:

Main Goal: Lose Fat, Tone Muscle

Workout Type: WORKOUT C - Giant Set Training

Training Level: Intermediate

Days per Week: 3

Equipment: Bodyweight, Dumbbells, Kettlebell

Warning—Your body is going to feel these more intense "Giant Sets," including your heart and lungs.

This is a great way to burn fat, tone muscle tissue, and save time. With your wedding now just weeks away, time saving and burning maximal amounts of fat are key.

Although "Giant Sets" may sound intimidating, this is the best way to burn fat and build lean body mass in the quickest amount of time.

Giant sets consist of 4-5 exercises in a row, with 12 reps each. You can combine as many exercises as you want, but if you want the Bridal Body, you have to hit everything.

Say hello to the Giant Set!

Giant Sets 101

If you've been following along, you've probably included these exercises in your routine weekly and you are already familiar with the concept of performing two exercises back-to-back with no rest in between (previously described as Interval Training).

Tri-sets take this a step further by grouping three exercises back-to-back.

Let's ramp it up a notch and go for four or more! Now, my friend, you have yourself a Giant Set!

The premise of a Giant Set is that you perform four or more exercises back-to-back, taking minimum rest between each. You can do all the exercises for one muscle group, have several exercises for a couple of body parts, or mix things up and perform a total-body Giant Set.

With the final countdown on, go big or go home! Go Giant Sets!

Benefits of Giant Sets

Weight training has an awesome metabolic effect. If you're a fitness buff and have spent any time reading about the iron game, you'll know about the massive impact weight training has on Excessive Post-exercise Oxygen Consumption (EPOC) and how the damage caused to your muscle fibers by lifting weights raises metabolic rate and calorie burn to a greater degree than cardio training. Well, with Giant Sets, this effect is amplified further as you're combining the anaerobic element of weight training with the aerobic nature of cardio.

Even if you are not a fitness buff yet, know this: You'll also burn more calories during your session than you would with a traditional weights workout involving straight sets and lengthy rest periods.

The result you'll achieve is faster fat loss.

As for muscle mass, Giant Sets not only increase your total training volume, but also raise your time under tension. Plus, if Giant Sets are a new addition to your training, this stimulus can be the catalyst for new growth.

Sounds awesome, right? So here's how you do it:

First up, decide whether you want to hit your whole body or just a certain area, and work out your repetition ranges.

For strength, you're looking at lower rep ranges with fewer exercises and a focus on performing explosive movements. There will be more of an emphasis on full-body training in this strength session, as this gives each muscle group adequate rest.

For hypertrophy (or muscle growth), we're talking more of a split-style Giant Set, with slightly higher reps to increase the time under tension on each muscle group.

For fat loss, both these approaches work great, and actually including both is your best option.

Keeping your wedding dress in mind, and an eye on the clock, we will hit everything at once!

We will keep the same exercises, adding in a few more—something old, something new...

Add:

1. Close Grip-Knee Tricep Pushups

2. Bicycle Crunches

3. Glute Standing Kickbacks

4. Plie Squats

5. and, for extra cardio, Mountain Climbers!

The following Giant Sets are designed to keep your heart pumping and muscles working while losing body fat!

3 days a week, 4 rounds each, and 1 minute of rest in between. Fast and furious!

Remember there are 12 reps per exercise with no rest between exercises.

You are only to rest 60-90 seconds in between the "Giant Sets."

Workout A

Set 1

15 Jacks

Pushup

Plank to Pushup

Squats

Set 2

30 Seconds Run in Place

Reverse Lunges

Standing Military Press

Tricep Pushup

15 Mountain Climbers

Workout B

Set 1

30 Second Jacks

Plank Hold 30 Seconds

Reverse Lunges

Crunches

Set 2

Mountain Climbers 30 Seconds

Plie Squats

Glute Kickbacks, 12 Each Leg Standing

Bicycle Crunches

Workout C

Set 1

30 Seconds Run in Place

Pushups

Plank to Pushup

Standing Lateral Raises

Set 2

15 Jacks

Squats

Bicep Curls

Dead lifts

Week's Workout

MONDAY	TUESDAY	WEDNESDAY	THURSDAY	FRIDAY	SATURDAY	SUNDAY
Training & Cardio	Cardio	Rest	Training & Cardio	Cardio	Training & Cardio	Rest

Let's get back to that rest. Make sure you rest at least one to two days in between workouts, and of course, if you're sore, wait another day. Drink plenty of water and remember this does NOT replace your fat-burning cardio.

Remember to track your progress on The Bridal Body worksheet on page 121.

So, how's your eating going? Remember you cannot out-exercise a bad diet or poor nutrition habits. The Bridal Body only works if you are working, and that includes eating right.

How are we changing the game with the big day approaching?

Protein—Because of the extra calorie spending and stress increase, let's keep protein at a minimum of one gram per body weight. This will allow for proper recovery, as well as keeping your metabolism from slowing down during caloric restriction. So, if you weigh 130 pounds, aim for 130 grams of protein per day at this level of training.

Fats—We still need this macro for metabolism, vitamin absorption, and healthy hair, skin, and nails. However, let's see if we can save 90 calories per day by reducing our intake to 10 grams from the 16 we were having. That would mean ½ oz. or 10 almonds, or a teaspoon of peanut butter or avocado. I know, it's a bit of a tease, but at this point we are looking at reducing calories specifically with our energy macros, and fats pack 9 calories per gram—so we have to cut the fat!

Carbs—Touchy subject! I will never cut this out completely, but now we have to cut back a little more. Remember, the energy sources are the macros that we use to maximize fat loss. If we do not use them, they get stored as fat. If we eat the right amount of them, at high training times we can utilize what we take in, as well as burning old glycogen and stored fat for fuel. That's the goal.

I'm going to cut back by a whole meal, leaving you 25-50 grams of starch carbs per day. That will reduce your calories per day by at least 100, and by the end of the week you will have cut 700! Not bad.

So a day will now will look like this:

Meal 1: Protein, Starch

Meal 2: Protein, Fruit or Fat

Meal 3: Protein, Veggies

Meal 4: Protein, Veggies, Fruit or Fat

Meal 5: Protein, Veggies

** Remember never mix carbs and fats!

So, if you choose to put your fruit at meal two, then eat your fat at meal four—or vice versa. Green veggies are unlimited!

*** Remember to stick to the condiments listed on our initial shopping list. Here's a reminder of Stacy's favorites: lemon/ lime juice, low-sodium soy sauce, coconut oil cooking spray, all vinegars, salsa, any spices or seasonings. And stay far, far away from the heavily processed salad dressings, sauces, marinades, and sprays.

A sample diet plan can look like this:

Meal 1: 4 egg whites, 1 slice Ezekiel toast, coffee or tea with skim milk or other non-dairy creamer

Meal 2: Apple, whey protein shake

Meal 3: 4 oz. tuna on a bed of lettuce, 1 cup green veggies

Meal 4: Whey protein shake, 1 tsp. peanut butter

Meal 5: 4 oz. chicken, 2 cups veggies, and a large salad

or

Meal 1: Whey protein shake and ⅓ cup oats

Meal 2: 3 oz. tuna, 10 cashews

Meal 3: 4 oz. chicken, 1 cup steamed kale or broccoli

Meal 4: Apple or ½ cup berries and whey protein shake

Meal 5: 4 oz. sirloin steak with 1 cup kale, unlimited salad

If you haven't worked your absolute hardest, do it now. I can't even tell you what a relief it was to reach my goal in the weeks before my wedding. When you go to your first fitting and put on your wedding dress and actually feel good in it, it just feels awesome. I felt beautiful and confident. Just a tip—I asked to have my last fitting as close to my wedding day as possible, just in case I lost any extra weight. (They agreed, and I did!) Again, reaching your goal in advance takes so much pressure off, then as long as you can maintain, you can focus on all of the other things you have to do, and oh, yes, your groom!

Side note- by following my lead, eating what I stocked in our house, and coming with me on walks, my groom lost his own 20 lbs! He looked and felt his best too.

Ohhh.. one more tip! This was a great piece of advice I received. Book your hair trial on the same day as your fitting, so you when you try your dress on your Bridal Body, you can truly get a sense of how you are going to look on your wedding day! (I actually decided to change my hairstyle after not loving how it looked with my dress at my fitting!)

ONE MONTH AWAY FROM YOUR BIG DAY!

It's hard to believe we are already here—but it's go time!

There's not a lot of time left to get to where you need to get, but let's hope you are pretty much there and can reach your goal in the next month. This month the focus is being as time-efficient and productive as possible with meal prep, training, and schedules. You must have your food prepared and ready to go with you to all of your appointments this month! There's no point in looking back, but if you did not adhere to the prior training/cardio and diet plans, you may not be ready for these new ones. So be realistic and always go back to the prior plans, if need be . But this upcoming month will surely get you in the best shape possible for your day! So let's see where you are.

Turn to page 12 and track your progress on your Bridal Body worksheet!

REWARD MEAL TIME! Yes, I said a reward meal, but within reason. You have been working your butt off, so it's time for a reward—but just one, and then back on the wagon. It's easy to let this get out of control, so if you think this will trigger more cheating or worse food, OPT OUT of the reward meal. If not, schedule with a friend or your soon-to-be spouse for a night on the town and enjoy yourself. I have no restrictions with this, and you can even throw in a dessert and an alcoholic beverage.

What we will need: Nothing new (just space to do your training, one gallon of water per day, and motivation!)

Meal Plan Specifications:

Eat Every Three Hours

Protein Every Meal

Water, Water, Water

No Processed Foods

Get Your ZZzz's

Best of the Best Macros:

Chicken, tuna, egg whites, tilapia, berries, apples, oats, brown rice, sweet potato, broccoli, spinach, kale, and asparagus!

All green veggies are unlimited!

In the Car Must-Haves:

Water Bottle

Almonds

Grilled Chicken

Rice Cakes

Lara Bars (these are all natural and the ONLY bars Stacy will allow!)

Cut up veggies, such as peppers and raw broccoli

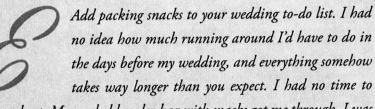

Add packing snacks to your wedding to-do list. I had no idea how much running around I'd have to do in the days before my wedding, and everything somehow takes way longer than you expect. I had no time to stop and eat. My good old cooler bag with snacks got me through. I was emotional enough as it was—being hungry and cranky would have made it much worse.

So we have been using three main variables to make progress and get in Bridal Body shape! There's been a specific cardio plan, training plan, and meal plan. These variables have changed as time passed and you progressed, and now all three will change again—some more than others.

Changing variables, as well as the timing of these changes, will have a lot to do with your progress. Remember, if you continue to do what you have always done, you will never change—and that applies to almost everything!

Let's Start with the Easy Part

Cardio Plan: This has been heavily weighted in, and will continue. Without target heart rate fat-burning cardio, we will lose out on burning essential amounts of pure fat that has been stored. The duration has been 30-40 minutes four times a week. I'm looking to challenge you to increase this to five times or even six times a week at 30-40 minutes per session, which will spend an extra 400-500 calories per week! That will be sure to help you lose the last few pounds you were looking to shed.

I know cardio can be pretty boring, so grab a friend. Elisa's new playlist will be sure to get you going, too!

Elisa's Playlist

Shake Señora Remix – Pitbull (featuring T-Pain, Sean Paul, & Ludacris)

Now That We Found Love – Heavy D & The Boyz

We Got the Beat – Go-Go's

Higher – Taio Cruz (feat. Travie McCoy)

Wild One – Flo Rida (featuring Sia)

Shake It Off – Taylor Swift

Hot in Herre – Nelly

Don't Call Me Baby – Madison Avenue

Stronger – Kanye West

Stronger – Britney Spears

Love Runs Out – One Republic

Gotta Get Through This – Daniel Bedingfield

Feel This Moment – Pitbull (featuring Christina Aguilera)

One More Time – Daft Punk

Carry On – Fun

Heartbeat Song – Kelly Clarkson

So hopefully your week will look like this:

Monday through Saturday: Cardio

or Take a day off during the week and do it all weekend!

Remember, this type of cardio is best done after training when all glycogen (sugar) from the muscles have been utilized, or on an empty stomach first thing in the morning so that you tap into stored body fat, not glycogen storage from daily food.

MONDAY	TUESDAY	WEDNESDAY	THURSDAY	FRIDAY	SATURDAY	SUNDAY
Training & Cardio	Cardio	Training & Cardio	Cardio	Cardio & Yoga Class if possible	Training & Cardio	Rest

The Wedding Week

Well, congrats!! You did it. It's your wedding week. Can you believe it?

If you have made it to your goal weight, I applaud you. I know it wasn't easy, but I know it was worth it. If you didn't reach your goal weight but are happy with your results and feel better and learned about fitness and nutrition along the way, I also applaud you.

And if you didn't get to exactly where you wanted to be, there's still a little time left. There are some last-minute tips that we can use to lose a few more pounds this week.

Keep in mind you will have the least amount of time this week and will need as much energy as possible, as well as sleep and proper nutrition.

I like to look at each individual case separately, so I devised an action plan for each of you.

It's important to recognize that worst thing you can do is stress more, sleep less, not eat well, and, god forbid, wind up sick on that special day. I want you feeling your best. So no matter what position you are in physically, remember there is only so much you can do now to lose any more weight, or look any better.

Elisa's Wedding Week Musts

5 DAYS BEFORE

MAKE A CHECKLIST

There will be a lot of unforeseen errands in the days to come. Make a list and decide on priority items, things that can be done a few days out, etc.

THE PAPERWORK

Who wants to think about contracts and legalities on their wedding day? Read them a few days before to be sure you have everything in place.

4 DAYS BEFORE

SET ASIDE TIP MONEY

On your wedding day, there will be a number of vendors to tip. Set aside your money in envelopes ahead of time. Ask your Maître D' any tipping questions in advance.

3 DAYS BEFORE

BEAUTY APPOINTMENTS

Try to space out your beauty appointments. Make your nail appt. 2 days prior to the big day! Pro tip: Gel manicures are reasonably priced and won't chip!

2 DAYS BEFORE

SLEEP & EAT

You may be nervous, excited or both the day before your wedding. Be sure to sleep & eat regardless of your pre-wedding jitters! You want to be refreshed and energized to enjoy the entire day.

1 DAY BEFORE

Remember to Hydrate!

Maintain your water intake. Keeping hydrated will keep you feeling full, keep bodily functions moving, help keep your skin looking fresh, and maintain weight or weight loss.

Keep the Vitamin C in!

As you know, this week is extra stressful. Make sure you still take your Vitamin C daily to keep immunity boosted. We do not need a run-down or sick bride.

Get Your ZZZzz's

Rest and recovery is key to continuing weight loss and will help you look refreshed on your big day. It will also help you stay healthy during this stressful week.

Exercise

I know you have a ton to do. Keep at least two days in this week. Not exercising at all may actually make you feel more sluggish. It may also cause you to fall off track in your diet.

Do Not Binge

Eating poorly can easily happen this week with guests in town, rehearsal dinners, late nights, and so much to do. You'll be in the car more, appointment hopping, so pack your snacks and stay away from the oh-so-convenient drive-through! You will be very surprised how fast five pounds and water retention can creep up on you. You want to be able to zip that gown and feel good.

Don't Skip Meals!

This is for metabolism, of course, but you do not want to feel famished, sluggish, or on the verge of passing out due to stress and lack of nutrition.

Keep the Protein in and Flowing

Remember that the power macro helps keep burning calories, maintains blood sugar, and keeps us full. Don't lose it.

Now for those individual strategies...

If You Reached Your Goal

Congrats! Yippee! I'm so happy for you, truly. This week you can literally glide on, as long as you keep the principles above in mind. Try to keep nutrition the same, and if you cannot do your workouts, you will maintain what you have anyway, so don't stress it. But if you can work out, go for it. You can probably use the stress relief. Just be careful not to do too much and lose a lot more, because we also do not need a dress that's too big. Sometimes the stress of the wedding week takes two to four pounds off a bride anyway, so be careful.

If You Are Just a Few Pounds Away from Your Goal

Okay, you have two choices: Try to lose 'em or be happy with where you are. I would hope at this point you had your last fitting and are set to go. This stressful week can help shed a few pounds off, anyway, but if you really want to ensure that the last couple come off, you need to maintain the last set of exercise programs and stay on the meal plan. No cheating or skipping meals, and no skimping in the training department. If you are happy where you are, then you can choose to keep at least two of the training days, as well as maintain the meal plan as best as you can.

Cut carbs in half by reducing starch intake. Your energy sources will decrease and more fat for fuel will be used.

Drink extra water with lemons—the acid in lemons is sure to detoxify you and help metabolize fatty acids. The extra water will also keep you fuller and aid digestion.

Drink a cup of Joe—adding in a little caffeine will help boost your metabolic rate naturally and also help you get in an extra workout!

Sit in a sauna—extra sweating equals extra weight loss.

If You Are Far Away from Your Goal

Well, first off, I'm sorry to hear this. I hope you are at least happy with your progress and what you learned overall. There are a few hints this week just to maintain your progress—eat your meals as planned, stay prepared, and stay with the principles listed above. You do not want to gain extra weight this week.

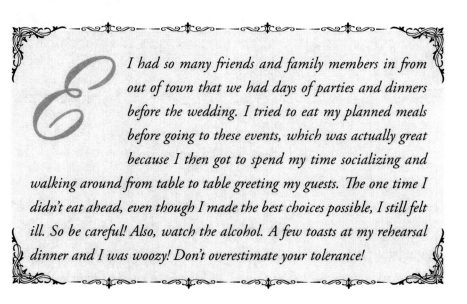

I had so many friends and family members in from out of town that we had days of parties and dinners before the wedding. I tried to eat my planned meals before going to these events, which was actually great because I then got to spend my time socializing and walking around from table to table greeting my guests. The one time I didn't eat ahead, even though I made the best choices possible, I still felt ill. So be careful! Also, watch the alcohol. A few toasts at my rehearsal dinner and I was woozy! Don't overestimate your tolerance!

The Day

If you are sleeping out the night before your wedding, don't forget to pack your food for the morning of your wedding day. While everyone else ate bagels at my mom's, I ate my regular food and snacks—and felt great. It was nice to have a "normal" on such an overwhelming day. The day gets crazy, so be sure to take time out to eat your lunch before you get dressed and leave for the ceremony. Despite swearing that I would, I didn't get to eat at my cocktail hour. So, I was very happy that I wasn't starving. My one big regret is that I was up late the night before my wedding and wish I had gotten more sleep. A good night's sleep would have been much more valuable than the last-minute things I was up doing. On the day of, something is bound to go wrong. My relatives showed up early; I was running late. And someone stepped on my veil and not only ripped it out of—and messed up—my hair, but ripped the veil itself. It was so torn up that my mother had to get out her scissors and cut off the bottom of it. Please, promise not to sweat the small stuff; it truly doesn't matter in the end. Keep reminding yourself what the day is really about: your love and your marriage.

It's here... The big day you've worked and waited for!

You have come so far from when we began, and now it's time to rest, relax, and let it happen. No matter what the goal was, you should feel good about your journey and your efforts. This was not only about looking your best, but hopefully you are feeling your best too. I believe no matter what happens, you are a new and better version of yourself.

Today keep drinking your water—carry that bottle with you—or heck, that's what a maid of honor is for! Eat breakfast (staying away from high-sugar foods in the morning is best, since you do not want to feel sluggish later). Also, you are not used to sugars, so be aware of what will happen if you choose to eat bagels, Danishes, or pastries first thing on your wedding morning.

Of course, you can always pack snacks, like almonds, rice cakes and chicken strips, but hey, it's just a suggestion. Your body should be used to eating every three hours, so make sure there is food there for you. No one wants a famished, cranky bride.

Dinner Is Served; Oh, and the Dessert Table!

I will not even hear of you not eating dinner and enjoying your dessert table. I'm not saying overdo it, or go bananas, but please eat! You deserve it. Enjoy it, savor it. You worked for it. There is no reason at all not to enjoy this wonderful meal with the special people who you chose to spend your day with. Bon appétit, and congratulations!

First of all, congratulations! I know how hard you've worked to achieve your Bridal Body, and plan a beautiful wedding. Now it's time to celebrate! Even with a ripped and cut-down veil, when I walked down that aisle, I truly felt like my best self. All of my hard work was worth it. I felt the healthiest and most beautiful I've ever felt—and when I saw my groom, the most loved. My last words of advice: Enjoy every second. The day goes so, so fast. As a friend advised me, stop for a second when you enter your reception and look out at all of the faces of the people who love and celebrate you; look at your husband, the love of your life, and take it all in. I've never felt so much love and happiness. I truly hope you feel the same. And, in case you are wondering, the wedding cake will taste even better than what you have been dreaming of!

Cake made with love by Oheka Castle Exec. Pastry Chef Daniel Andreotti

BRIDAL BODY WORKSHEET

	pre-Bridal Body	end of Workout A	end of Workout B	end of Workout C	final Bridal Body result
DATE:					
WEIGHT:					
BODY FAT PERCENTAGE (your local gym should be able to help you out):					
MEASUREMENTS:					
DRESS SIZE:					
ACCOMPLISHMENTS:					
CHALLENGES:					

Recipes

Healthy Chicken Cobb Salad

Yields 4-6 servings

Ingredients

8 cups mixed greens

2 cups chopped chicken, grilled

1 cup chopped celery

1 cup chopped cherry tomatoes

2 eggs, hard boiled and cut

2 Tbsp. green onions

1 cup crumbled blue cheese

½ avocado divided

Feta (optional)

Preparation

1. Fill a large bowl with salad greens; arrange the chicken, celery, tomatoes, avocado, and eggs on top of the salad. Top with green onions and cheese of choice. Use balsamic vinegar.

Healthy Stuffed Peppers

Yields 4 servings

Ingredients

4 medium green, yellow, or red peppers, washed and gutted

12 oz. ground turkey

1 cup chopped peppers, onions, and carrots, shredded

1 cup diced tomato

salt and pepper to taste

Preparation

1. In a saucepan, brown onions, peppers, and carrots with diced tomato for five minutes. Add the ground turkey and brown for 10 more minutes all together. Use salt and pepper to taste to add flavor! After the turkey is almost finished, turn the pan off and set the oven to 350 degrees. Place the peppers in a baking dish and add 4 oz. of the turkey combo to each pepper. Fill to the top. Bake for 30 minutes or until brown on top.

Turkey Meatball Soup

Yields 4 servings

Ingredients

1 lb. ground turkey breast

2 cups cooked brown rice

2 Tbsp. fresh thyme, chopped

¾ tsp. kosher salt, divided

½ tsp. freshly ground black pepper, divided

6 garlic cloves, minced, divided

2 large egg whites, lightly beaten

4 tsp. extra-virgin olive oil

½ cup chopped onions

½ cup chopped celery

½ cup chopped carrot

6 cups trimmed, chopped lacinato kale (about 1 lb.)

¼ tsp. crushed red pepper

5 cups water

Preparation

1. Preheat oven to 400 degrees.

2. Combine turkey, ¼ tsp. salt, ¼ tsp. black pepper, 2 garlic cloves, and egg whites in a large bowl; mix gently just until combined. Working with damp hands, shape turkey mixture into 16 meatballs (about 1 oz. each).

3. Place all meatballs on oven-ready baking dish that has been sprayed with non-stick spray. Place 1 cup of water in dish with meatballs. Bake for 8 minutes.

4. In a soup pot over medium heat, add 2 tsp. olive oil, carrots, shallots, and celery to pan; sauté 5 minutes. Add remaining 4 garlic cloves; sauté 1 minute. Add kale, ½ tsp. salt, ¼ tsp. black pepper, and red pepper; cook 2 minutes, stirring occasionally.

5. Add water; bring to a boil. Add meatballs to pan. Reduce heat; simmer 10 minutes or until kale is tender and meatballs are done.

6. Portion half a cup of rice into each bowl. Spoon soup over rice, assuring that each portion has 4 meatballs to account for appropriate protein intake.

Egg White Frittata

Yields 6 servings

Ingredients

1 tsp. olive oil (for cooking vegetables, if desired)

Assorted vegetables (chopped, diced, or shredded to desired size) Onions, bell peppers, jalapeno peppers, scallions, mushrooms, tomatoes, spinach, sun-dried tomatoes, zucchini, fall squash, garlic, etc.

24 egg whites

Sea salt & pepper to taste

Optional ingredients: Red pepper flakes, herbs, spices

Preparation

1. In a large skillet on medium heat, drizzle olive oil and sauté onion and garlic for about 4 minutes, until tender and fragrant. Set aside. If you prefer to have a crunch in your vegetables, feel free to cut them into small pieces and place them in the pan raw.

2. In a large bowl, whisk together eggs, salt, and pepper. Continue whisking until foamy.

3. Place sautéed (or raw) veggies in a pie dish lightly sprayed with oil, and pour egg mixture over top, making sure to evenly coat all the veggies. Cover loosely with foil and bake in the oven at 425 degrees for about 10 minutes. Reduce heat to 350 and continue baking for 25 minutes. You'll know it's done when a knife inserted comes out clean. Enjoy! (Cooking times and temperatures may vary depending on pan; if using a thin pizza pan, cook at 400 degrees for about 7-8 minutes, then reduce to 350 for an additional 10-15 minutes. This time is an estimate due to oven variability.)

Protein Muffins

Yields 12 servings

Ingredients

1 cup mashed bananas (the more ripe the better!)

2 cups old-fashioned or rolled oats

4 egg whites

4 scoops whey protein (any desired flavor, with a 25g protein scoop)

1 Tbsp. agave

Pinch salt

1 tsp. vanilla extract

½ cup carob chips

Preparation

1. Preheat oven to 380 degrees.
2. Mix all ingredients together and let sit while you prepare the muffin pans.
3. Spray a muffin pan with non-stick spray.
4. Divide batter into 12 muffin cups. Bake 20-25 minutes. You'll see the edges just starting to brown, and the muffins will be firm to the touch. The muffins may stick when hot but will remove easily when cooled for a bit.

Whole-Wheat Pizza Margherita

Nutrition Facts per Slice

237 calories

7g total fat (2g saturated)

0mg cholesterol

31g carbohydrate

12g protein

5g fiber

703mg sodium

Serves: 8

Details:

Sometimes nothing satisfies like a slice of cheesy pizza. This one's made with a whole-wheat crust and part-skim mozzarella, so it's ideal for post-workout meals, or just to enjoy a healthy slice of pizza.

Ingredients

Crust:

1 package (1/4 oz.) active dry yeast

1 cup warm water

1 Tbsp. extra virgin olive oil

2 tsp. salt

2 ½ cups whole-wheat flour, plus additional for kneading

Dash of cornmeal

Topping:

2 large tomatoes, thinly sliced, then cut into half circles

8 oz. part-skim mozzarella, thinly sliced into half circles

Extra virgin olive oil (optional garnish)

8 fresh basil leaves, thinly sliced

Preparation

1. In a medium mixing bowl, combine yeast and warm water; let sit until yeast foams, about 5 minutes. Stir in oil and salt. Add flour, ½ cup at a time, mixing with a large spoon, until dough comes away from the side of the bowl and holds together.

2. Sprinkle additional flour onto work surface. Turn out the dough and knead about 5 minutes, until it is smooth and springy, adding only enough flour to keep it from sticking to the board.

3. Form dough into a ball; place in a medium bowl. Cover with plastic wrap and put in a warm place. Let rise until doubled in size, about 2 hours.

4. To make pizza: Preheat oven to 475 degrees. Place dough on lightly floured work surface; flatten with your hand. Using floured rolling pin, roll dough outward from the center. Form dough into a circle or rectangle about ¼-inch thick.

5. Sprinkle pizza stone or baking sheet with cornmeal. Lay crust on stone or sheet. Lay alternating slices of tomato and cheese on top of the crust, slightly overlapping each piece. Lightly drizzle with additional oil, if desired.

6. Let pizza rest 10 minutes. (This step can be skipped, but it makes for the crispiest crust.) Place pizza in oven and bake 20 minutes, or until cheese is melting and browning a bit. Sprinkle pizza with sliced basil leaves

Low-Carb, High-Protein Pizza Recipe

Now, I know everyone has his or her favorite cheat meal, and for me it's pizza. I've loved it since I can remember. As you know, I love coming up with healthier versions of all kinds of foods, and this is my low-carb, high-protein pizza recipe. Like all my recipes, you can adjust the ingredients and amounts to fit your own daily macros and personal taste.

Ingredients

1 large whole-wheat pizza dough (pre-made or from my other dough recipe)

2 Tbsp. tomato purée

3 cans low-sodium diced tomatoes

3 cups part-skim mozzarella cheese

2 cups spinach or broccoli

3 mushrooms

½ green pepper

1 green chili

180g chicken breast (approx. 7 cutlets)

Basil

Garlic Salt

Paprika

Preparation

1. Weigh out your chicken breast, season, then cook in the oven as you normally would for 40 minutes.

2. Take a whole-wheat crust and add 3 cans of diced tomatoes.

3. Add some low-fat cheese and veggies of your choice (I added spinach, chilies, mushrooms, and green pepper).

4. Add 180g of cooked chicken and top with low-fat/fat-free mozzarella, then sprinkle on herbs/spices of your choice (I added basil, garlic salt, and paprika).

5. Cook under the grill until the cheese has melted and the base has gone crispy (5-7 minutes). Enjoy!

Nutrition Facts per Slice (in an 8-slice pie)

52g carbs

6-9g fats

28g protein

Approx. 400 calories

SIDE OF WHOLE-WHEAT PENNE WITH LIGHT MARINARA

¾ cup dry whole-wheat penne (or 1 cup cooked)

1 cup diced tomatoes

1 tsp. olive oil

Salt

Garlic powder

Onion powder

Pepper

Combine all ingredients.

Nutrition Facts

230 calories

6g total fat

6g protein

42g total carbohydrate

6g sugars

Low-Fat Greek Tzatziki Dip

32 oz. container low-fat Greek yogurt, strained in a coffee-filter-covered colander

3-4 pickling cucumbers

2 tsp. fresh garlic, minced

½ tsp. salt

1-2 Tbsp. extra virgin olive oil

Juice of half a lemon

Fresh minced dill, to taste

Combine all ingredients.

Low-Fat Cucumber and Tomato Salad

1 cup sliced red tomatoes

1 cup sliced yellow tomatoes

½ red onion, chopped

½ red and yellow pepper, chopped or cut

1 whole cucumber, peeled and cut

Combine all ingredients, then drizzle with balsamic vinegar, salt, pepper, and dill to taste.

RED WINE SPRITZER

1 bottle of red wine

16 oz. cranberry juice

1 liter of seltzer

Combine everything in a punch bowl. Garnish with ice and cubed pear and strawberries.

RED WINE COOLER

2 apples, cubed & frozen

2 pears, cubed & frozen

1 bottle desired red wine

1 liter seltzer

Prepare fruit and freeze. Mix wine and seltzer; garnish with frozen fruit.

PROTEIN PANCAKE

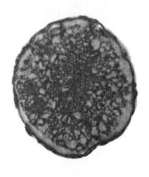

½ cup plain rolled oats

1 scoop of your favorite protein powder

1 egg white

4 oz. water

Cinnamon

Mix all together and fry in a pan coated with non-stick spray.

Nutrition Facts

25g carbs

27g protein

3g fats

1g sugar

Acknowledgements

To my parents who always pushed me to be my best and achieve my goals and dreams, and are always there when I need them.

The Weight Room Plus, I thank you for all your support over the years and your help with The Bridal Body Book project.

Maria Faller, my right hand, my assistant and now my friend. I could never have made it through the final phase of this project without you.

To my best friends, Raquel, Maxine, Bambi, Carmen and Anne, I love you all and thank you for helping me get through the toughest but best time of my life.

Matthew Miglio, where do I begin? First, thank you for referring me to Lori Ames at the PR Freelancer. I am so grateful for your patience, support, friendship and love throughout this process. Thank you for your contributions to my writings and for always being by my side.

Thank you to Isabella Lebeouf from Be Beautiful hair and makeup for making me feel even more beautiful!

To my client and friend Michelle Medoff, for your love and loyalty and for introducing Elisa & I.

To all of my brides, it has been my pleasure working with you to achieve your Bridal Body. Nikita Bonamo, Jennifer Gray and Erin Corcoran, thank you for your contribution to this book.

To all of my clients, thank you for your understanding and support during this busy Bridal Body book writing process. I am so proud to work with each and every one of you!

~ Stacy

Mom & Dad, for all of your love, support, encouragement, and for always making me believe that I could achieve anything I put my mind to- and work for. Oh, and for making me so many special meals on the Bridal Body plan! To my sister & Matron of Honor Diana and brother & Man of Honor Thomas for being the best friends and siblings I could ever ask for.

Thank you to my loving family and my News 12 family, I am so blessed to have you all by my side cheering me on. To my UTA Bienstock team and my agent, confidant, and trusted friend, Lia Aponte, thank you for always believing in me.

To my friend Michelle Medoff, thank you for introducing me to Stacy and encouraging me on my Bridal Body journey. To Dr. Jeannette Graf and Georgene Grella for giving my skin the bridal glow and for your friendship. Thank you to my bridal beauty team, Suzanne Feynman & Caitlin Hallbert.

To Geri Ainbinder for your time, all of the training, and for pushing me and never giving up on me and my pursuit of The Bridal Body! To Anne Bratskeir for helping me find "the dress" and for capturing the moments in photos! To my friends at Oheka Castle for helping me plan the wedding of my dreams. To Andres Echo Diaz & Echo Events for making my wedding even more memorable.

And once again to my husband, Mo Cassara- my light, my love, my partner on this incredible journey.

And to everyone who followed our wedding blog "OurSomethingNew. com" and sent me notes of encouragement, thank you from the bottom of my heart.

~Elisa

Thank you to Dennis Hansen & Dennis Hansen Images for your time, talent and photos in this book.

Thank you to Echo Events & Jack Roman Photography for the beautiful wedding photos.

Thank you to Lori Ames & pr Freelancer for your guidance.

Thank you to Justin Sachs & our Motivational Press Family for all of the time and love that went into making The Bridal Body book.

Please find more fitness and nutrition tips, videos,
recipes and Bridal Body products on our website
BridalBodyBook.com.

Join in the conversation and share your
#BridalBody journey on:

f   **/BridalBodyBook**

⊙   **@BridalBodyBook**

𝕐   **@BridalBodyBook**

𝓟   **/BridalBodyBook**